Big Data for Qualitative Research

Big Data for Qualitative Research covers everything small data researchers need to know about big data, from the potentials of big data analytics to its methodological and ethical challenges. The data that we generate in everyday life is now digitally mediated, stored, and analyzed by web sites, companies, institutions, and governments. Big data is large volume, rapidly generated, digitally encoded information that is often related to other networked data, and can provide valuable evidence for study of phenomena.

This book explores the potentials of qualitative methods and analysis for big data, including text mining, sentiment analysis, information and data visualization, netnography, follow-the-thing methods, mobile research methods, multimodal analysis, and rhythmanalysis. It debates new concerns about ethics, privacy, and dataveillance for big data qualitative researchers.

This book is essential reading for those who do qualitative and mixed methods research, and are curious, excited, or even skeptical about big data and what it means for future research. Now is the time for researchers to understand, debate, and envisage the new possibilities and challenges of the rapidly developing and dynamic field of big data from the vantage point of the qualitative researcher.

Kathy A. Mills is Professor of Literacies and Digital Cultures, Institute for Learning Sciences and Teacher Education, Australian Catholic University, Brisbane. A prolific, award-winning academic author, ethnographer, and Future Fellow of the Australian Research Council, she is also Chair of the American Educational Research Association Writing and Literacies Special Interest Group and serves on a number of international journal editorial boards.

"Big data is flooding society. In this important and original volume, Kathy Mills shows that big data nicely fits with qualitative researchers' pursuit of naturalistic materials. Essential reading for researchers and students."
> *David Silverman, Emeritus Professor, Sociology Department, Goldsmiths' College, London University, Visiting Professor, UTS Business School*

"In the world of social research, there have until now been two paradigmatic kinds of methodology, broadly classified as qualitative and qualitative. Rarely the twain shall meet, except by awkward juxtaposition in 'mixed methods'. Now Kathy Mills introduces us to a completely new species of research which is at once qualitative and quantitative. *Big Data for Qualitative Research* is a concisely described and elegantly argued account of the new qualitative data sources, from social media digital learning environments. Massive in their scale, these sources of social evidence require innovative methods, so opening new avenues for analysis and lines of interpretation."
> *William Cope, Professor, Department of Education Policy, Organization & Leadership, College of Education, University of Illinois, Urbana-Champaign*

Big Data for Qualitative Research

Kathy A. Mills

LONDON AND NEW YORK

First published 2019
by Routledge
2 Park Square, Milton Park, Abingdon, Oxon OX14 4RN

and by Routledge
52 Vanderbilt Avenue, New York, NY 10017

Routledge is an imprint of the Taylor & Francis Group, an informa business

© 2019 Kathy A. Mills

The right of Kathy A. Mills to be identified as author of this work has been asserted by her in accordance with sections 77 and 78 of the Copyright, Designs and Patents Act 1988.

All rights reserved. No part of this book may be reprinted or reproduced or utilised in any form or by any electronic, mechanical, or other means, now known or hereafter invented, including photocopying and recording, or in any information storage or retrieval system, without permission in writing from the publishers.

Trademark notice: Product or corporate names may be trademarks or registered trademarks, and are used only for identification and explanation without intent to infringe.

British Library Cataloguing-in-Publication Data
A catalogue record for this book is available from the British Library

Library of Congress Cataloging-in-Publication Data
Names: Mills, Kathy, 1974– author.
Title: Big data for qualitative research / Kathy A. Mills.
Description: Abingdon, Oxon; New York, NY: Routledge, 2019. | Includes bibliographical references and index.
Identifiers: LCCN 2018060194 | ISBN 9780367173814 (hardback) | ISBN 9780429056413 (ebook)
Subjects: LCSH: Qualitative research. | Big data.
Classification: LCC H62 .M4425 2019 | DDC 001.4/2028557—dc23
LC record available at https://lccn.loc.gov/2018060194

ISBN: 978-0-367-17381-4 (hbk)
ISBN: 978-0-429-05641-3 (ebk)

Typeset in Times New Roman
by codeMantra

This book is dedicated to Ryan, Lachlan,
Juliette, Marie and Henry

Contents

Foreword ix
Acknowledgments xi

Introduction 1

1 What is big data? 6
Aims of this book 7
Chapter snapshot 8
Defining big data 9
Big data examples 11
Impact of big data on research fields 12
Big data and digital life 12
Limits and assumptions of big data 13
Big data beginnings for qualitative research 14

2 Big data in historical context 16
Defining data 16
Big science and small science 17
Beginning of big textual data 17
Big data: Coining and use 18
Uses of big textual data today 19
Knowledge politics and the history of big data 21

3 Challenges of big data for qualitative researchers 22
Challenges of working with big data 25
Complexities of data privacy and ownership 27
Challenges of big data acquisition 27
Challenges of BDA 31

4 Potentials of big data analytics for qualitative researchers   34
Text mining 35
Opinion mining or sentiment analysis 38
Information and data visualization 40
Netnography 41
Follow-the-thing methods 43
Mobile research methods 44
Multimodal analysis 45
Rythmanalysis 46
Conclusion 47

5 Big data ethics, privacy, and dataveillance   49
Privacy and dataveillance 50
Consent 52
Implications 54
Conclusion 56

6 Anticipating big data futures for qualitative researchers   57

References   61
Index   75

Foreword

Many of the emerging insights of qualitative research with respect to big data—and in particular, as this book points out, the application to big data of established ideas of what constitutes data "quality"—actually mirror what many quantitative researchers, especially medical and social statisticians, are also concerned about. Dataset size, while helpful in many ways, does not guarantee either relevance or enhanced understanding. Indeed, in many cases, the often uncontrolled and haphazard manner in which big data are acquired requires new approaches to their analysis. Moreover, because of the size of the datasets, there is a strong need for quantitative and qualitative researchers to work jointly. In the past, for example, the analysis of texts has utilized quantitative techniques and "models" via quantitative coding techniques, and this now is likely to become much more important. This book lays out a set of scenarios around big data for consideration by the qualitative research community, and quantitative researchers too will have a lot to learn from a reading of it.

It is possible to argue that, just as much of the traditional quantitative research space occupied by statistical professionals is being infiltrated by computer scientists from outside the traditional research community, so these and similar professionals, with their expertise in algorithmic design, will increasingly invade the sphere of qualitative research, thus making it all the more urgent for qualitative practitioners to immerse themselves in a deep understanding of quantitative and digital approaches. A salutary lesson can be found in the so-called "Google flu" episode (Lazer, D., Kennedy, R., King, G., Vespignani, A. The Parable of Google Flu: Traps in Big Data Analysis. *Science* [New York, NY]. 2014, p. 343), where search terms associated with incipient flu symptoms, using data derived from Google's search engines, were associated with subsequent flu epidemics in the USA. This appeared to work extraordinarily well for a few years in providing early warnings of epidemics until it catastrophically failed. One of the lessons of this is that the reliance on predictions with a lack of any strong theoretical understanding of causal relationships between human behavior and real-life outcomes is dangerous, and this book elaborates on this. Both quantitative and qualitative researchers should beware the "bigger is better" message. Kathy Mills has an interesting discussion of issues such as these and some of the more outlandish claims of big data "proponents" and usefully sets big data in its historical context.

This book also tackles the difficult issues of data sharing and privacy. With increasing public awareness of dubious data sharing practices for commercial and political purposes, data privacy groups are emerging with the aim of protecting individual rights and increasingly legislation is being formulated. The effects of this on public willingness to provide data and the ability of researchers to access it are discussed in a welcome attempt to raise awareness and discussion of such issues. Likewise, the ownership of data and the apparent unwillingness of data custodians such as Google and Facebook to allow access to any but their own researchers raise important social and ethical issues, and these too are discussed.

This book deals at some length with textual analysis, which is becoming increasingly attractive to many researchers with the digitization, systematization, and prevalence of analytical tools applied to very large texts, whether transcripts of public events or generated from samples of individuals. The book also discusses applications in the analysis of subjective attitudes, visualizations, and ethnography. A whole chapter is devoted to big data ethics, especially consent and privacy. The author raises the issue of interest conflicts when data are inevitably harvested by commercial or governmental organizations during the course of citizens' daily activities, such as communication with friends or buying goods. What does consent mean in these circumstances? The author also mentions the "anonymization" problem, where attempts to release data anonymized to the extent that they are relatively safe from a malicious "attacker" trying to uncover a particular individual's data, can easily lead to the data being so "degraded" that it is unfit for analysis purposes.

The book ends with speculation about the future of big data for qualitative researchers, and a plea for such researchers to become fully involved in understanding what is happening, working with quantitative researchers in the process, and being prepared to learn new methodologies.

This is a clearly written introduction to this important topic, with useful references to existing work. It should be on the reading list for all those concerned with big data, not just qualitative researchers.

Harvey Goldstein
London
November 2018

Acknowledgments

I acknowledge the anonymous international peer reviewers (blinded), who volunteered their expertise to provide critical and constructive feedback that was invaluable in shaping this monograph.

I also acknowledge Ms Lesley Friend and Dr Ryan Mills who edited every chapter of the pre-submitted manuscript with great attention to detail. I thank Dr Bessie Stone who edited the reference list of the pre-submitted manuscript.

This research is supported in part by an Australian Research Council Linkage Grant (LP 150100030) funded by the Australian Government. The views expressed herein are those of the author and are not necessarily those of the Australian Government or the Australian Research Council.

Introduction

Big data is evolving at the intersection of technology and changed social realities. The early waves of a hardware revolution have provided much needed data architectures that are now catching up on software developments ("Big data needs a hardware revolution", 2018). Big data has appeared in discourses of marketization, touted as a "new class of economic asset", comparable even to gold and currency (Lohr, 2012, p. 1). Yet scholars with critical insight see big data as a phenomenon that has technological, cultural, and scholarly dimensions (boyd & Crawford, 2012). Some have called it a "big data movement" (Parks, 2014, p. 355), underscoring the ideological nature of big data debates. While the term "big" implies that the enormity of the data is important, most researchers agree that size alone is an insufficient descriptor of big data and that its networked or connected nature is an essential feature.

Big data arguments have drawn attention to the fact that a significant proportion of human social interaction today is "informationalized"—generated and relayed through digital information networks, leaving data traces of social interaction that are often geolocated and timestamped (Cope & Kalantzis, 2015, p. 196). Such traces of data are becoming ubiquitous, prompting researchers to observe the sheer magnitude of human social data (Cope & Kalantzis, 2015). At the same time, a key feature of much big data is that they are by-products of social interactions and processes for which the main purpose is not for social research (Shlomo & Goldstein, 2015).

The first mentions of big data were often focused on its computational affordances. The words of Gary King, director of Harvard's Institute for Quantitative Social Science, have resounded, "The march of quantification, made possible by enormous new sources of data, will sweep through academia, business and government. There is no area that is going to be untouched" (Lohr, 2012, p. 1). Soon after, big

2 Introduction

data was quantitatively described as a "newfound ability to crunch a vast quantity of information, analyse it instantly, and draw sometimes astonishing conclusions from it" (Mayer-Schonberger & Cukier, 2013, p. 1). Others, such as Lohmeier (2014), acknowledge that, in some ways, big data is a natural continuation and progression of scientific developments over the past 100 years rather than a giant leap.

Numbers aside, text-based data are similarly amassing at an unparalleled scale, holding considerable potential for qualitative researchers to utilize for important questions about human and social behavior (Golder & Macy, 2011; King, 2011). In their work, boyd and Crawford (2011, p. 5) have raised the vital concern that, "big data risks reinscribing established divisions in the long running debates about scientific method". This book is a response to this fermenting problem by reclaiming the potentials of big data for qualitative and mixed methods researchers who have been marginalized in the discourse. A current search of articles, books, and book chapters that seek to address big data specifically for qualitative research, reveals few works of significant length (see for an exception: Hand, Hillyard, Pole, & Love, [2014]).

From the perspective of division among fields of research, scholarly critiques point to the lack of take-up among social scientists, and cultural sociologists in particular, who have largely left the potentials of big data in society "to computer scientists, who possess the technological expertise to extract and manage such data, but lack the theoretical direction to interpret their meaning" (Bail, 2014, p. 467). There are now very few text-based data that are not digitally archived, and analyzing textual data has been a strength of many qualitative approaches to methodology (Bail, 2014). Qualitative researchers, who have traditionally researched society and culture on the ground, can understand the potentials and constraints of relevant social data from the internet, sensors, mobile phones, wearable technologies, and more, in order to address the pressing questions of our times.

This book is intended for anyone who has a stake in the use of data, whether for knowledge, research, business, learning, management, health, security, science, social science, cultural studies, anthropology, geography, data archiving, data infrastructure, higher education, policy, and more. Most notably, it seeks to make big data meaningful to qualitative and mixed methods researchers. Qualitative researchers, such as ethnographers, as well as mixed methods teams, are working with increasingly large and digitalized data sets. It is becoming less common to research alone, relying on handwritten field notes. Conversely, it is becoming more common for researchers to use digitally mediated interviews, recordings and transcriptions, video observations, online or offline data produced by participants, digital archives and search engines, data visualizations, and digitally supported coding and analysis. Data and metadata are becoming thicker, as each recording is time-stamped and each interaction with participants comes with metadata that is more accurate than one's memory.

Nevertheless, qualitative and mixed methods researchers largely remain skeptical of dataism—the assumption that technology can always do better than humans. They do not assume that technically generated data is more objective or more reliable, nor does "bigness" render obsolete the need for robust theory to interpret the data. Some argue that the real value of big data research might be realized when large digital, networked data sets are combined with qualitative research methods (Lohmeier, 2014). For example, research of the purposes for using Twitter could be supported both by the analysis of Twitter feeds and by observing and talking with a manageable number of Twitter users to understand their insider perspectives (Marwick, 2014).

Examples of significant qualitative research engagement with big data include the work of Ignatow and Mihalcea (2013), who proposed a model for big data analysis that synthesizes neuroscience and Bourdieusian practice theory (Bail, 2014). Researchers have combined big data generated from research-purposed mobile phones for college students, with ethnographic fieldwork performed by a participant observational anthropologist who collected "thick" ethnographic fieldwork data on friendship and social relations (Blok & Pedersen, 2014).

In another example, Smith, Cope, and Kalantzis (2017) mapped what is recorded digitally as we write using various technologies, to show how traces are generated and recorded, and how those mechanisms can matter in tracing learning in education. They demonstrate the profound implications for understanding communication, once we recognize that almost all new literacies, such as video and image sharing, gaming, blogging, posting, and responding to posts, involve social skills developed through collaboration and networking in online spaces (Jenkins, Clinton, Purushotma, Robinson, & Weigel, 2006).

Ethnographers and other qualitative researchers study in a big data world of mediatization—that is, where social life is mediated indirectly or directly by digital technologies (Lohmeier, 2014). While qualitative researchers have regarded certain geographical or organizational sites and fields as a focus of observation, ethnographies in a big data world may define a range of digital spaces as a field, whether web sites, forums or online communities. Yet even the traditional ethnographer who participates alongside the researched in relationships of trust finds that when they leave the field, the field relations do not end, because relations are not neatly bounded by physical sites (Lohmeier, 2014). At the same time, despite the digitization and mediatization of life, objects and the sensorial nature of culture and society are still highly significant and should not be ignored. Digital and online research needs to account for the interaction between what is done online and the material parts of the interactions that involve bodies and tangible keyboards in geographical locales.

A key point then is that a big data world is gradually changing the multisited, material or immaterial, flexible, multimodal, and multi-mediated nature of qualitative research. These transformations call for qualitative researchers to be ready to make shifts in research data collection, analysis, archiving, and sharing, and to be open to thinking about, discussing, and doing research differently where it can advance knowledge. At the same time, big data researchers need not become preoccupied with the research affordances of data-driven approaches to the point that they fail to ask the most relevant research questions.

Current debates about big data and its potentials and limitations for qualitative research can be informed by what is known about the general methodological problems and transformations brought about through digitization. For instance, there are changes to the nature of texts, media, objects, and means of qualitative research, including the shape of research communities, technological architecture, and regulatory bodies that influence how research can be conceptualized, conducted, shared, and valued (Hand, 2014).

Even if researchers do not wish to engage in big data analytics, the pervasiveness and rapid advance of big data technologies are already having an impact on the way qualitative research is conducted, evaluated, and shared. For example, the affordances of qualitative coding software are expanding, and funding bodies often place increasing weight on large-scale qualitative research which is seen as having greater rigor, impact, and national benefit than studies with small numbers of participants (Camfield, 2018). Qualitative research can be done at various scales, yet researchers have drawn attention to the importance of the quantity as well as the quality of the data. Williams and Morrow (2009, p. 578) suggest that the "quantity of data is key" to supporting the categories or themes, to understand their richness and complexity, and to strengthen the trustworthiness of the findings.

Importantly, complementing the computational emphasis in much big data research, this book is a recognition of the value of small data. As boyd and Crawford (2012, p. 7) argue, "Research insights can be found at any level, including at very modest scales. In some cases, focusing just on a single individual can be extraordinarily valuable... in some cases, small is best". Qualitative researchers are united in the view that working with enormous data sets does not define good research (Lohmeier, 2014, p. 79). Likewise, Borgman (2015, p. xviii) puts the everyday nature of data in perspective:

> Data rarely are things at all. They are not natural objects with an essence of their own. Rather, data are representations of observations, objects, or other entities used as evidence of phenomena for the purposes of research or scholarship...big data is not necessarily better data.

The real significance of research is largely a consequence of asking the right research questions. Most importantly, whether big or small, the real worth and value of data is realized in its use (Borgman, 2015).

1 What is big data?

We are living in an era of massive digital change that is transforming the fundamental nature of communication and the way we research. The prevalence and potential of big data has captured the imagination of public media since early articles in *The Economist* (Cukier, 2010) and The *New York Times* (Lohr, 2012). Premier scientific journals, such as *Nature* ("Community cleverness required", 2008) and *Science* ("Special online collection: Dealing with data", 2011), launched special columns dedicated to the discussion of big data. Big data across a broad range of fields is collected, analyzed, stored, and disseminated digitally. These changes have contributed to a variety of responses, ranging from the amplification of big data promise, to digital angst about ethical and productive ways to exist amid digital change and disruption. What constitutes appropriate use of big data in contexts of increasing global multiplicity of texts, information, and facts?

The digitalization of data is becoming ever more apparent, functioning in transformational ways in everyday life for individuals and organizations. Digital data is particularly salient given the broadened range of communication channels, media, and social media. Data is now generated rapidly from a variety of sources, such as social media and video feeds, mobile devices, radio frequency identification readers, genome sequences, medical databases, software logs, and wireless sensory networks (Fuller, Buote, & Stanley, 2017). The main big data types commonly cited include social media data, transactional data, administrative data, sensor data, and personal data, such as from tracking devices (Shlomo & Goldstein, 2015).

Big data is generating immense interest from researchers, research grant funding bodies, industries, marketing companies, and beyond. Researchers may find the terminology and analytic methods associated with big data confusing, such as data mining, machine learning, sentiment analysis, and deep learning. In addition, there are new methods of text, image, audio, and video analytics (Fuller et al., 2017). Across many disciplines, researchers can no longer ignore the big data hype, as many seek to know how big data practice can transform the future of fields that use both quantitative and qualitative research methods, and to determine whether new analytic methods for big data can help to answer different kinds of research questions in innovative ways.

Even if qualitative researchers may not need real-time analytics to answer questions urgently, there is an unprecedented quantity of textual data beyond the internet that is potentially useful to qualitative researchers, such as digital copies of almost every book published (e.g. Google Books), news archives and newscasts (e.g. Proquest), legislative reports and discourses (e.g. National Archives of the United States and Great Britain), podcasts, historical audio sources, local town hall meetings, interviews, and field notes [e.g. Dataverse Network or Economic and Social Data Service (ESDS) Qualidata]. There are increasingly fewer types of text, image, and speech-based data that are not being archived by someone (Bail, 2014). Qualitative researchers typically invest large amounts of time manually organizing and coding textual, image, and video data, while qualitative data may be transformed into quantitative data to apply data mining and visualization techniques (O'Halloran, Tan, Pham, Bateman, & Vande Moere, 2018).

Aims of this book

This book addresses the roles of both big data and qualitative research in a world in which there are data of massive breadth across so many fields and spheres of human activity. Within the academic community, some have argued that big data renders small-scale research, commonly used in the social sciences and humanities, potentially at risk (Alberts, 2012; Berlekamp, 2012; Mayer-Schonberger & Cukier, 2013). If social and behavioral data that were previously the locus of much qualitative research have been "datified" (Strong, 2013), is the role of the qualitative researcher losing a significant foothold? Before researchers blindly follow big data trends, questions need to be asked about the accessibility, ethics, utility, costs, and limits of big data. What is the scale of analysis necessary to understand phenomena in the particular area of research interest?

Is the use of big data incommensurate or diametrically opposed to the values of the qualitative researcher? Should big data and qualitative research be seen as complementary and suited to particular types of social questions and problems? What exemplars do we have to support the integration of qualitative methods with big data in

8 *What is big data?*

mixed methods research investigations, which integrate the combined strengths of quantitative and qualitative interpretations to address research problems? This small book on big data debates both the limits and potentials of big data for qualitative researchers. After historically contextualizing big data in Chapter 2, it outlines a range of big data methods and analytic tools that are increasingly of interest to qualitative researchers in Chapter 3. The potentials and pitfalls of big data are examined, including assumptions about who has access to big data and who misses out. Chapter 4 explores big data methods and analytics, with an eye towards new developments for qualitative researchers. Later chapters discuss issues of ethics and privacy in a risk society, such as surveillance and data ownership. Together, the chapters explore some of the potentials of combining the strengths of big data with those of qualitative research, such as combining automated tools for the analysis of big data with the interpretative theories or cultural frames of reference generated through qualitative research. Such approaches can use qualitative research to contextualize the social milieu in which the data were produced (Mills, 2017).

Throughout the volume, I address critical questions, debates, and perspectives of big data trends, unearthing both the promises and challenges. This is vital given current and future opportunities for big data applications, and conversely, new concerns about ethics, privacy, surveillance, and secondhand digital data use, on the other. The use of data, whether big or small, must account for the burgeoning array of data forms that extend well beyond numerical data to include multimodal data—data that includes combinations of words, images, audio (e.g. sound effects, music, voice recordings), moving images (e.g. video), and three-dimensional designs. The notion of big data has inspired, excited, confused, frustrated, and provoked researchers worldwide as digital media render voluminous data sets more readily discoverable, distributable, open to scrutiny, and more efficiently able to generate answers to the questions that researchers ask (Mills, 2017).

Chapter snapshot

This chapter will define and debate the role of big data for researchers, while considering the questions that big data poses for qualitative researchers. Too often, data experts do not acknowledge the different roles and values of researchers who work in fields with little data, rare data, or even with no data (Borgman, 2015). To qualitative researchers,

What is big data? 9

data can include vastly diverse traces of human activity across a variety of modes and media—data which is often not primarily numerical (e.g. video, photographs, conversations, 3D printing, drawings, tapestries). Thus, to the qualitative researcher, big data might appear on the surface to be somewhat irrelevant. However, qualitative researchers are increasingly conscious that scholarship occurs in a digitally networked world (Borgman, 2018), and most qualitative data can be rendered, analyzed, archived, and shared digitally. The digital transformation of information and communication technologies means that qualitative researchers are not insulated from the changes that are opening up new efficiencies, larger data sets, quicker analysis, and new ways of answering important questions. Some disciplines have been slower than others to recognize and harness the potentials of new big data analytics, such as sentiment analysis, machine learning, and techniques for big data visualization.

Defining big data

What exactly constitutes big data, and how do qualitative researchers come to terms with this phenomenon? There are almost as many definitions of big data as there are theorists. For example, some simply define big data as "enormous datasets" that may be structured, semi-structured, or unstructured (Chen, Mao, & Liu, 2014), while others argue that the main emphasis to date in much of the literature is on unstructured data (Dedić & Stanier, 2017). The size of big data is constantly changing with technological advances, rendering the use of terabytes or exabytes to define big data as an inexact science. Regardless, there is agreement that big data are diverse, complex, and massive in scale, requiring specialized analytic tools and technologies to capture, process, and reveal insights in a timely way (Hashem et al., 2015).

Many specify the characteristics of big data using the three V's: volume, velocity, and variety (Chandler, 2015; Laney, 2001). Volume refers to the mass scale of data, although theorists acknowledge that the relative scale varies across different disciplines. The current volume of big data is historically unprecedented, and increasing every year (Fuller et al., 2017).

Velocity refers to the rapid generation of data or timeliness. Examples of high-velocity applications include machine sensory monitoring in production lines, satellite imagery, credit card fraud detection, wearable data, parcel tracking and other global positioning applications,

10 *What is big data?*

social media feeds, customer web browsing, power usage data, and clickstream analysis of web user data to recommend products and target advertising.

Variety addresses the various modalities or types of structured, semi-structured, and unstructured data, which may include numerical data, textual data, audio, images, and so on (Chandler, 2015). Integrating different types of data from multiple sources can potentially address new questions. Using multiple data types is called data fusion—this may produce more accurate, complete, and contextualized information than what can be achieved through analyzing as single type of data.

Others have added a fourth V—value—which refers to the need to extract the often-covert value from enormous, rapidly generated data sets of various types (Chen et al., 2014). Still others have added a fifth V—veracity—meaning the quality of the data or low "noise" in the data. A shift in any of these dimensions can influence the scale of research and scholarship (Fuller et al., 2017).

Distinguishing between big and not big is problematic, because data can be big in a multitude of ways—such as what can be done with them, the insights that they reveal, and the scale of extraction and analysis required to make them useful (Borgman, 2015). The challenges of managing data of significant volume, velocity, and variety have actually been discussed since the turn of the twenty-first century, including debates about 3D data (Laney, 2001). The term "big data", however, was only added to the Oxford Dictionary in 2013, defined as "data of a very large size, typically to the extent that its manipulation and management present significant logistical challenges" (cited in Borgman, 2015, p. 6).

I define big data as rapidly generated, digitally encoded information of significant volume, velocity, variety, value, and veracity: Data that is used as valued evidence for a phenomenon, and which often has relationality with other networked data (Clarke, 2016; Mills, 2017). Big data needs analyses to be useful for scientific work or knowledge production, and a common feature of big data is the associated logistical challenges of its analysis, manipulation, reduction, and management, due to its enormity.

It is also important to consider what is meant by the contested term "data" in scholarship. The term "data" refers to "entities that are used as evidence of phenomena for the purpose of research" (Borgman, 2015, p. 29). Entities include any variety of forms of information suitable for interpretation—from material objects, such as sculptures, artwork, and drawings, to digital data, such as digital images, textual data, and numerical information. When referring to entities, data is used in the plural form, except when referring to data as a concept.

It is important to recognize that data are not truths in themselves, but rather, are facts or sources of evidence that are used to support a claim about reality (Borgman, 2015).

Big data examples

Digital data, such as third-party cookies, web and marketing analytics, on-site web engagement analytics, GPS tracking, and other tracking technologies, are like footprints marking time and place, creating ongoing records of social communication, and location activity (Mills, 2017). Common types of big data can include traces of human activity captured on social media, learning analytics, business and operational data, web and mobile analytics, streaming data, commercial and government data, and sensory data from the Internet of Things or IoT. Other applications of big data include visualizations of large data sets, machine learning, sentiment analysis, opinion mining, computer-assisted content analysis, natural language processing, and automated data aggregation and mining (Lohmeier, 2014; Parks, 2014). For example, Google manages one of the largest sources of big data, enabling analysis by the public through the open access tool, Google Insights. Apple, Twitter, and Facebook also keep big data, with some companies granting researchers access to subsets of data, such as iScience Maps™ for Twitter (Reips & Garaizar, 2013).

Social media sites generate large bursts of data of current relevance about a significant, but inexhaustive number of users. Screen-scraping refers to the extraction of information from internet sites, and data is collected and used for social purposes that range from gene sequencing to consumer behavior, and from learning analytics to predictive analytics (Bail, 2014; Siegel, 2013). The spread of mobile technologies has assisted the scope of these and other kinds of big data, with higher numbers of devices owned by family units and users throughout most parts of the world (Borgman, 2015).

Digital data are becoming computation intensive and data intensive, and its manipulation often requires significant logistical challenges (Meyer, 2009). The IoT is increasingly becoming an important source of big data, as sensory technologies become more consistently used to collect usage and environmental, geographical, logical, and astronomical data. Mobile devices, transportation facilities, public facilities, and home appliances are becoming data acquisition technologies that are connected to the IoT. Currently, internal data owned by enterprises are the main sources of big data (Chen et al., 2014).

Impact of big data on research fields

So which research fields have taken up big data? The research potentials of big data have been explored in a growing number of fields that include political science (Clarke & Margettes, 2014), global league tables in education research (Crossley, 2014), learning analytics (Rockwell & Berendt, 2016), immigration control and border security (Ajana, 2015), business scholarship (Frizzo-Barker, Chow-White, Mozafari, & Ha, 2016), and civil strife management (Nardulli, Althaus, & Hayes, 2015). Stock market shifts are traced in communication scholarship (Bollen, Mao, & Zeng, 2011), while patterns in children's media cultures have also been observed (Montgomery, 2015).

Big data has been used for forensic social science in sociology (McFarland, Lewis, & Goldberg, 2016), applications in human geography (Kitchin, 2013), disaster response and recovery (Ragini, Anand, & Bhaskar, 2018), monitoring disease trends in public health (Paul & Dredze, 2011), and e-cometrics (O'Brien, Sampson, & Winship, 2015), to name a few. New research fields, such as digital humanities, have burgeoned in the big data era (Bail, 2014). Fields such as astronomy, genomics, physics, macroeconomics, and digital humanities tend to work with very large volumes of data, while a large number of scholars in some fields conduct research with minimal amounts of data (Borgman et al., 2016; Sawyer, 2008). This is by no means an exhaustive list, as newer forms of big data analysis, such as text, video, image, and learning analytics, are emerging globally.

Big data and digital life

As a consequence of the internet and the associated mobile technologies, big data is networked, connected, and traceable, but more difficult to analyze with conventional statistical analysis software (Snijders, Matzat, & Reips, 2012). Big data researchers aim to harness the potentials of computational capability and algorithmic accuracy to mine, examine, engineer, and employ extensive digital data sets to discover new findings about phenomena. In some quarters, the use of big data is undergirded by the epistemic assumption that big is better, offering increased sophistication, power, and forms of intelligence—a claim that has been challenged by qualitative researchers and other existing literature (see, e.g., boyd & Crawford, 2011).

While the world appears to be overflowing with big data, or the so-called "data deluge" highlighted by the *Economist* in the article "Data Everywhere" (Cukier, 2010), what is significant is the assumption that big

What is big data? 13

data-driven knowledge is changing the way in which knowledge is generated, analyzed, shared, or governed (Chandler, 2015). In areas such as international relations, discussions have centered on the possibilities for solving problems of international scale through applications of knowledge generated by access to big data. These include prevention and timely responses to natural disasters, global conflict, climate change, disease management, and other societal problems that transcend national boundaries in globalized societies. For example, research published in *Nature* used the frequency of Google search engine queries to track outbreaks of influenza (Ginsberg et al., 2009). More recently, researchers have argued that along with epistemological and ontological assumptions of big data, we need to engage with more fundamental concerns regarding privacy and surveillance, data access, ownership, and civil liberties (Chandler, 2015).

Limits and assumptions of big data

In their work, boyd and Crawford (2011) have contended that big data has emerged as an interplay of three features:

i   technology available to maximize computation power and algorithmic accuracy to gather, link, and compare large data sets;
ii new possibilities for analysis of large data sets to make claims; and
iii a widespread belief that large data sets offer a higher form of intelligence or knowledge that can generate insights of truth, objectivity, and accuracy that were previously impossible.

This third point is important because it addresses the epistemic assumptions about the nature of truth and how to acquire it that provided fertile ground for big data hype. Examples of such outlandish beliefs held by earlier proponents of big data are illustrated in claims of Berry (2011, p. 8): "Instead of philosophy…computationality might be understood as…an ontological 'epoch' as a new historical constellation of intelligibility". Others include Anderson (2008), Editor in Chief of *Wired*, who argues of the "petabyte age":

> This is a world where massive amounts of data and applied mathematics replace every other tool that might be brought to bear. Out with every theory of human behaviour, from linguistics to sociology. Forget taxonomy, ontology, and psychology. Who knows why people do what they do? The point is that they do it, and we can track and measure it with unprecedented fidelity. With enough data, the numbers speak for themselves.

14 What is big data?

Anderson's infamous commentary is extremely provocative, since he belittles the theory-generating role of whole disciplines (e.g. psychology, linguistics, and sociology) in guiding research, and the emphasis on research that seeks to examine human motivation. It epitomizes the unchecked assumptions that often pervade big data hype. It ignores the tendency towards confirmation bias—the use of analytics to support or favor preexisting beliefs. It also fails to acknowledge some of the biggest obstacles to using big data, such as the almost ubiquitous lack of information about the social contexts in which the data is produced (Griswold & Wright, 2004).

Small data researchers have called for the need for strong theory to ensure the big V-value of big data is realized. Bail (2014, p. 465) argues, "while computer scientists have produced powerful new tools for automated analyses of 'big data', they lack the theoretical direction necessary to extract meaning from them". While computer scientists perhaps cringe at such blanket criticism of their discipline, a key point is that big data research can potentially benefit from the input of theoretically and qualitatively oriented researchers. Likewise, qualitative researchers can benefit from the expertise of big data computer scientists, statisticians, and informatics experts to address new research questions with rapidly generated, varied, and larger-scale data. Selected methods of collecting, analyzing, and interpreting any type of data depend largely on the expertise of researchers in the domain (Borgman, 2015).

Big data beginnings for qualitative research

Researchers are beginning to challenge the status quo, theorizing new epistemologies and practices of big-small data research, similar to what many now describe as quali-quantitative research (Latour, Jensen, & Venturini, 2012). For example, the Copenhagen Social Networks Study has explored this nexus by integrating ethnographic and computational methods to investigate the social relations and friendships among 1,000 students, drawing on the experience of interdisciplinary research teams that combine sociologists, physicists, anthropologists, computer scientists, and economists (Blok & Pedersen, 2014).

The large team of more than 25 researchers made continuous recordings of the freshman class using smart phones supplied to the students. The researchers tracked face-to-face encounters via Bluetooth, geo-location proximities using GPS, social network data via apps, and telecommunication data via call logs. They combined this big data with ethnographic fieldwork performed by a participant-observational anthropologist within the freshmen group who collected "thick" ethnographic fieldwork data on friendship and social relations (Stopczynski, Sekara, & Sapiezynski, 2014). The findings examined how friendships, networks, and behaviors form, offline and online, and insights about how the researchers themselves study "big data" and "small data" in a single project, including how they handled issues of ethics and privacy.

The point is that big and small data methods are not mutually exclusive, and indeed, researchers are combining them in productive ways. While qualitative researchers are often reluctant to give much credence to the big data hype, in some disciplines at least, there may increasingly be an element of truth in Wang's (2013, p. 1) caution that "ethnographers must engage with big data for fear of being minimized as a small line item on a budget, relegated to the 'small data' corner". Stoller (2013, p. 1) argues that "The problem of big data is here to stay, which means that in the coming months and years we'll need a legion of ethnographically trained analysts to produce 'thick data' to save us from ourselves".

2 Big data in historical context

Even before the advent of the printing press, a deluge of information was described in the ancient biblical text, "Of the making of books, there is no end..." (Ecclesiastes 12:12). Census data was used for governance by ancient Babylonians in 3800 BC. Fast forwarding to 1887, Herman Hollerith invented an electric machine that read holes punched into paper cards to tabulate the 1890 USA national census data. This innovation reduced the census data processing time to one year instead of eight (Friedman, 2012). What might be surprising to some is that big data is not an entirely new concept, and the current distinction between big data and small data is not as sharp as commonly described. This chapter provides a brief background of the big data phenomenon and locates earlier developments and uses of large textual data sets, as well as the more recent rise of big data rhetoric. It sketches the trajectory of contemporary growth in big data research, and the social and technological shifts that have contributed to its currency.

Defining data

Before charting the rise of big data, it is useful to locate the similarly popular, but often taken-for-granted plural term "data"—which dates back to 1646 in theological scholarship. The use of the term has been in a constantly upward trajectory from the seventeenth century. Borgman (2015) observes that data was involved either as a set of principles accepted as the basis of an argument, or facts, particularly those taken from Scripture. Data did not pertain to scientific or mathematical evidence gathered through observation or experimentation until the late eighteenth century. The term "data" is now in its fifth century of use, and has taken on multiple meanings that shape and are shaped by advances in digital technologies (Borgman, 2015; Rosenberg, 2013).

Big science and small science

Contemporary big data debates are somewhat analogous to the differentiation in the 1960s about big science and small science (Borgman, 2015). As coined by De Solla Price (1963), "big science" is comprised of collaborative efforts by groups of researchers who exchange knowledge both unofficially and officially across the globe. Rather than referring to the measurable size of scientific research ventures, the modifier *big* principally denotes the maturity of science. In contrast, *little science* refers to small-scale work by many individual researchers or small teams—work that produces findings, theories, or methods to address particular research problems for a community or locale. Little science is often more flexible to include novel and varied methodological approaches, and these are typically locally analyzed and owned (Mills, 2017).

Beginning of big textual data

While we are currently witnessing a "big data movement" (Parks, 2014, p. 355), past data sets (e.g. census data) were collected and analyzed, and were much larger than some current examples of big data. Diary studies in qualitative research have a long history of very large-scale and often longitudinal use, such as the Mass Observation project of 1937 to the early 1950s (Bancroft, Karels, Murray, & Zimpfer, 2014). This decades-long, large-scale research program documented the minutiae of everyday life in Britain through a national consortium of diarists of varied gender. The research team collected the diaries in monthly intervals, and the diaries differed greatly in form, length and detail. These extensive narrative or textual records of significant scope and duration afforded a remarkable and insider view of early twentieth-century British life and culture (Bancroft et al., 2014; Mills, 2017).

Another early example of qualitative or narrative data collected on a massive scale is the International Time-Use Study of 1965, by Szalai (1972), in which enormous volumes of data were rapidly generated from 2,000 participants. The adult participants, ages 18–64, from 12 countries kept continuous logs to map their individual time use over the course of each day. The original logs were later expanded to connect other large data sets on budget, spending, wages, transportation, leisure, and other dimensions of economy and time. These kinds of big data diary studies continued into the late twentieth century, including project SIGMA—Socio-sexual Investigations of Gay Men and Aids (1986–1994) by Coxon and colleagues (1993), that gathered 1,035 narrative diaries to chronicle the changing lifestyles of gay men in response to HIV infection (Mills, 2017).

While the "digital turn" (Mills, 2010) has rendered manual, large-scale recording of daily activities virtually obsolete, situating the groundswell of interest in big data within a historical context demonstrates that the largeness of big data is not the main development. Data sets generated through large networks by research participants have a long history. A key difference today is that huge amounts of data are routinely collected and stored digitally. Thus, what distinguishes big data from these earlier large studies is that it is often not intentionally engendered by researchers to test a theory, because big data wrangling—the extraction, cleaning, and transformation of unrefined (and often messy) data sources—often, though not exclusively, aims to gain insights from existing data after the data has already been rapidly generated and stored (Boehmke, 2016; Chandler, 2015; Mills, 2017). Data collection to most researchers, whether qualitative or quantitative, is an expensive, time-consuming investment, and the potential to access big data naturally holds great appeal. However, the use and reuse of existing data, owned by one or more enterprises, involves political, ethical, and epistemic questions about data production, privacy, access, and ownership (Bancroft et al., 2014).

Big data: Coining and use

While the use of large data sets clearly has a long history, the use of the term "big data" is relatively recent. According to commentaries of the 1980s, the 1830s and 1840s were associated with an "explosion" of numbers, which made statistics an essential feature of data analysis, particularly for nation-states and governments to classify citizens (Porter, 1986). One of the earliest works on this topic, though again, prior to the use of the term "big data", is Hacking's (1991) piece on the history of statistics. He reflects on an "avalanche of numbers" and a "sheer fetishism of numbers" (p. 192). His late twentieth-century commentary similarly identifies a data deluge that occurred during the 1820s to the early 1840s.

Tracing the changing esthetics of information, analytics, and the place of media in constitutions of knowledge from 1945 to the 1970s, Halpern (2015) critiques an important shift in the moral values and esthetics of data including debates between modern and prewar conceptions of truth and certainty, and soon after, the embracing of communication and cybernetics. For example, after the Second World War, information inundation was often associated with totalitarian regimes. Since the 1970s, satellite-based surveillance systems, such as those produced by MacDonald, Dettwiler, and Associates (MDA), have been turned into a multibillion dollar commodity and the commercialization of outer space (Willis, 2016). Alongside developments in computing, these technologies have contributed to increasingly precise and efficient data mining and surveillance for astronomy, telecommunications, meteorology, navigation, space exploration, and other "panoptical" architecture for global surveillance (Foucault, 1977).

At the turn of this century, there was a renewed interest in accounts of the use of statistics for governance and control of populations, such as in the lectures of Foucault (2007) on security and territory, Desrosières (2002) on the politics of large numbers, and Elden (2007) on governmentality and calculation (Beer, 2016). Social commentator Hacking (1991) contended that the "statistics of populations...form an integral part of the industrial state" (p. 183). Postmodernity is characterized by unprecedented archiving of cultures and populations (Featherstone, 2000), while (often misplaced) faith in big statistics has contributed to new regimes of truth about society (Beer, 2016). As Beer (2016, p. 3) contends, "The collection of statistics is a great bureaucratic machinery...itself part of the technology of power in a modern state".

Notably, big data have been supported by infrastructures and modes of governance of the state, and with the rise of the internet, corporate, commercial, and social data gathering. Thus, while the term "big data" is recent, particularly the emphasis on the rapid generation of enormous and varied social and digital data, it extends previous eras of information expansion. The information deluge has conceptually become a data deluge, and data are seemingly revered as information (Beer, 2016; Borgman, 2015). This follows an epistemic shift towards statistics and observation, and an historical preoccupation of states and organizations with governance, territories, and surveillance, intensified in scale and scope through computing infrastructure, satellite-based innovations, and commercial interest (Ajana, 2013; Beer, 2016; Kitchin, 2014). The vast accumulation of big data and the development of technical infrastructure to support it are perhaps less striking than the ideological assemblages that prop up its commercial, legal, and economic power.

Uses of big textual data today

Criticism of the big data concept aside, qualitative researchers in the twenty-first century are collecting and curating increasingly larger and more varied nonstatistical data, such as digital images and text, multimodal data, websites, web diaries or logs (blogs), online chat, tweets, geospatial data, and screen casts (digital recordings of computer screen output). The prevalence of mobile devices, wearable technology, bring your own technology (BYOT) education programs, and user-generated web 2.0 content has opened up new potentials for research participant engagement in producing naturalistic data. Video recording, though sometimes perceived as a more intrusive form of observation, produces multimodal data of far greater detail than written field notes, and requires greater uploading, transcription, analysis, and digital archiving capacity. Digital qualitative analysis and archiving of narrative data must adapt to "new forms of data as they appear" (Borgman, 2015, p. 21). Much "thicker data" can be generated more rapidly by potentially larger numbers of participants than in the past, such as through crowdsourcing, calling for new computer-assisted ways to reduce and analyze big qualitative data.

Consider computation history—an approach that uses new computational tools with a variety of digital source materials to open up novel ways of understanding historical documents and narrative data. To overcome the costs and inefficiencies of individual qualitative researchers manually reading rafts of historical documents, computer programs can more rapidly search text and make connections to augment data analysis. Other historians have experimented with digitally visualizing the vast amounts of data—such as from shipping logs—enabling viewers to see geospatial trajectories over time (Hoffmann, 2013).

Another key development in qualitative big data is crowdsourced research, such as distributed video ethnography. These are collaborative forms of research in which multiple participants collect naturally occurring observational data, such as asking youth to record their everyday literacy practices using wearable cameras (Ronksley-Pavia & Barton, 2017), or activity tracking using participants' smart devices. Methods in which participants contribute to data collection have existed since the days of the large-scale diary and mass observational studies of the 1930s–1950s described earlier in this chapter. New digital technologies have removed some of the organizational, technical, and logistical barriers previously associated with distributed research, while also reducing some of the costs and time for the practical labor of field work (Bancroft et al., 2014).

Methods of crowdsourcing, from geographical mapping to web 2.0 participation, actively involve participants in the research process to democratize big data practices. A recent example of crowdsourced qualitative research "at a distance" is the Operation War Diary project, which involved users transcribing and classifying British Army war diaries from 1914 to 1922. Research participants become "citizen historians" who used the Zooniverse platform to classify diary pages, tagging them with names, places, unit information, weather, activity, casualties, and other information, translating potentially unstructured information into a sortable data set (Bancroft et al., 2014).

Knowledge politics and the history of big data

In sum, accounts of the history of big data are sometimes contradictory. For example, Letouzé (2012) claims that the big data revolution is a very recent phenomenon—less than a decade old. In such de-historicizing accounts, big data is presented as a clean, dramatic historical break or relatively discrete historic point in which the growth of data became exponential. Others do not posit a clean, historic break, but as demonstrated here, map both the recent use of the term "big data", and its historical antecedents and development, including its positive and negative consequences for research, individuals, and society (Burns, 2015; Elwood & Leszczynski, 2013). Knowledge politics pervade any account of the history and making of big data, including assumptions about what counts as big data, to what social ends they are used, and whose interests they serve.

3 Challenges of big data for qualitative researchers

It has been recently claimed that "the world's most valuable resource is no longer oil, but data" (*The Economist*, 2017). The growing big data literature and research points to both the challenges and possibilities of using this so-called "digital oil" (Yi, Liu, Liu, & Jin, 2014) for research and other academic or corporate purposes (Sivarajah, Kamal, Irani, & Weerakkody, 2017), while specific directions and applications for qualitative research are still emergent (Mills, 2017). In recent times, new benefits of big data analytics (BDA) have been advanced and demonstrated in relation to text mining in the humanities (Rockwell & Berendt, 2016), sentiment analysis of tweets (Yu & Wang, 2015), and visual analytics in undergraduate health education (Vaitsis, Nilsson, & Zary, 2014). Online software has been developed to generate a range of machine-enabled data on students' written compositions for educational practice and research applications (Smith, Cope, & Kalantzis, 2017). Methods and software have been proposed in social semiotics to integrate qualitative multimodal analysis with data mining and visualization (O'Halloran, Tan, Pham, Bateman, & Vande Moere, 2018). In educational research, a wide range of writing and learning environments and online tools are used to capture and collate learning process data (Knight, Shum, & Littleton, 2014).

When purposefully realizing these potentials, researchers are also navigating the logistical challenges, costs, and responsibilities. Some of the commonly observed difficulties include the complexities of integrating multiple data sources (Gandomi & Haider, 2015), a lack of knowledge, and an insufficient number of skilled personnel or data scientists (Kim, Trimi, & Chung, 2014). Others have pointed to difficulties keeping pace with new data infrastructure requirements (Barbierato, Gribaudo, & Iacono, 2014), such as scalable and flexible technologies to manage substantial amounts of data, whether textual or multimedia (Sivarajah et al., 2017). In terms of data management, there are new issues for ownership, authenticity, privacy, security, data governance, and data and information sharing (Barnaghi, Sheth, & Henson, 2013; Sivarajah et al., 2017). This chapter extends recent debates about the challenges and potentials of BDA for qualitative researchers who work with digital data. Qualitative researchers are well positioned to generate research questions that can be productively answered by large textual data sets, often having trustworthy repertoires of analytic methods to reduce, analyze, combine, interpret, and theorize multiple data sets across modes and media (Mills, 2017). Cultural sociologists, for example, who often gather unstructured, qualitative data *in situ*, have drawn attention to the slow uptake of big data in certain fields, despite its suitability for qualitative analysis:

> Inattention to big data among cultural sociologists is...surprising since it is naturally occurring—unlike survey research or cross-sectional qualitative interviews—and therefore critical to understanding the evolution of meaning structures in situ.
> (Bail, 2014, p. 467)

The collection of naturally occurring big data could be conceived as a different type of naturalistic inquiry—a hallmark of much qualitative research (Silverman, 2015). In naturalistic or qualitative inquiry, phenomena are often studied in their natural setting, and researchers aim to understand the social and cultural world from participant perspectives and observations of everyday social life. Big data is often unstructured, digital data that occurs as a byproduct of social interaction, including transactional, organizational, governmental, educational, or security processes, to name a few "patches" of contemporary social life. Another feature of big data that is consistent with qualitative research is an emphasis on rich or thick textual and image data, such as tweets, posts, blogs, chats, websites, legislation, e-books, news reports, and archived town hall meetings—potentially valuable narrative data suitable for qualitative analysis (Mills, 2017).

It is important to note that qualitative research is not homogenous or monolithic, but includes a diverse array of methodologies, each with their distinctive strengths. For example, participatory action research (PAR) positions the action researcher in relation to personal practice, while striving for research to be democratic and empowering— potentially life-enhancing for the participants (Gibson, 2002; Koch, Selim, & Kralik, 2002; MacDonald, 2012). The utilization of big data for PAR must attend to these important criteria. One way to achieve the emancipatory goals of participatory research with large data sets would be to use distributed ethnographies and other crowdsourced research in which participants contribute to data collection about their own social practices. In this way, the use of crowdsourced data could benefit significantly from the application of PAR principles and vice versa.

There are many applications that can be installed on personal mobile devices to self-monitor and track activities, and which can be reflected upon to empower the future decision-making of research participants. For example, apps that monitor heart rate, activity, nutrition, sleep, mindfulness, and location-based data can be used to be reflexive about personal health, and to inform personal goal-setting and change. Most strands of qualitative research can potentially make greater use of relevant text-based data across a range of modes that proliferate online, with an increased array of digital devices and data dashboards documenting everyday social activities.

Mixed methods research teams can combine big data analysis with case studies—combining interviews, focus groups, or participant observation with large-scale social media data—to make connections between rich data from individual users and large data trends. For example, social network analysis, a form of BDA, emphasizes the relationships among interacting units that facilitate flows of information. It has been used to map where these flows occur and to point to disruptions or ruptures in these networks (Mills, 2017; Todd, 2008). In separate studies, qualitative researchers have conducted multisite ethnographies to understand relational ties, illustrating how the online networks of adolescents are typically friendship driven (Ito et al., 2008; Mills, 2017). Mixed methods designs could combine such methods to address different dimensions and scales of social action.

The use of such complementary data sets can also inform the selection of mathematical models, such as those used to understand the micro-process of social media networks (Snijders, Matzat, & Reips, 2012). Bringing together teams of qualitative researchers with big data analysts could further elucidate the social basis or micromechanisms of online social tie-formation, such as how they differ for particular individuals, groups, and networks across different social media platforms. Essentially, qualitative research is useful for generating and refining theories to explain social and community practices. Data always belong to somebody, whether they are big or small. Most big data is constructed *in situ* and can be recovered accordingly (Christians & Carey, 1989; Mills, 2017).

There are potentials for taking a small data approach to research questions that aim to understand the motivations and beliefs of social actors, and combine it with the study of big data patterns of online, geo-spatial, or social behavior. For example, Google tracks what users search for, Twitter captures what social actors share, and Amazon monitors what people purchase (*The Economist*, 2017). Conventional qualitative methods, such as ethnographic interviews and on-the-ground observations, can help to interpret how big data is produced *in situ*, from a smaller, but repeated number of cases, such as in homes, schools, workplaces, and recreational sites. In this way, context-specific qualitative analysis of social practices and participant perspectives can be combined with BDA to enrich understandings of participant views to narrativize big data's general trends, together mapping and elucidating the dynamics of social networks (Lohmeier, 2014; Mills, 2017).

A potential contribution of the qualitative researcher is to investigate the underlying micro-processes that contribute to network characteristics or patterns in big data. Without the insights of qualitative researchers, algorithms and models are often developed on the basis of calculability, manageability, and numerical explanation, without an orientation towards robust theories of social or behavioral processes (Snijders et al., 2012). Similarly, BDA can show online user trends, the location of activities, or what users purchase, but it cannot explain why users access certain sites and make certain purchases, or access participants' subjective perceptions and feelings about their purchasing practices (Borgman, 2015; Mills, 2017). Qualitative methodologies can augment and adapt principles of BDA to attend to the implicit meanings and motives that undergird strings of words, images, and other digital artifacts to illuminate the cultural scripts through which humans understand and act upon their world (Bail, 2014).

Challenges of working with big data

Certainly, big data is radically changing the way research is done in some disciplines, and there is a clear shift towards the development of research infrastructure, products, and services to account for big data trends (Mills, 2017). Across many scholarly communities, digital data have become more rapidly generated, stored, mined, and distributed (Borgman, 2015). However, theorists have also pointed to some key caveats, some of which are discussed here and in Chapter 5 (privacy, surveillance, and ethics) of this volume. Previously, boyd and Crawford

(2012) and many others (Baym, 2013; Clarke, 2016; Perera, Ranjan, Wang, Khan, & Zomaya, 2015; Philip & Bilyana, 2017; Trottier, 2014) have raised concerns:

> There is a deep government and industrial drive toward gathering and extracting maximal value from data...information that will lead to more targeted advertising, product design, traffic planning, or criminal policing. But we do think there are serious and wide-ranging implications for the operationalization of big data, and what it will mean for future research agendas.
>
> (boyd & Crawford, 2012, p. 13)

It is worth considering whether or not big data means better data for the purposes to which the data will be used. Borgman (2015) uses the long-tail metaphor to characterize the availability and use of big data across research sectors. Data used by a small number of big scientists working at the head of the curve tend to use large volumes of homogenous data, similar in content, form, and structure. For such standardized data, it can be economically beneficial to develop shared infrastructure, data, tools, and services. However, small scientists at the end of the tail typically work with data that is characterized by greater variety, comprising heterogenous content, structures, modes, and materials of representation. Qualitative researchers are typically more able to adapt unique research methods and analytic tools to the data at hand. Much high-quality research and scholarship today is still conducted by individuals or small research teams who work with relatively small amounts of research funding and conventional methods to address exploratory cases of a more local nature, and which often utilize site-based observation on the ground. In such cases, the value of shared infrastructure and data, as well as large data sets, are often not as evident.

In addition to the field-specific divides in the application of big data research and BDA, there are clear geographical trends emerging, with China currently and significantly leading the way by the total quantity of published research on big data, followed by the USA, Australia, UK, and Korea, respectively. However, the USA leads the way in business scholarship of big data (Frizzo-Barker, Chow-White, Mozafari, & Ha, 2016). Countries that have been slower to undertake and disseminate research of big data and BDA include Belgium, Czech Republic, Denmark, Hong Kong, Norway, and Russia, perhaps pointing to the beginnings of a global divide (Sivarajah et al., 2017).

Complexities of data privacy and ownership

Several scholars have raised the complex problem of data ownership that arises in many uses of big data for research (Kaisler, Armour, Espinosa, & Money, 2013; Nath, Liu, & Zhao, 2007; Sivarajah et al., 2017). These authors cite examples from social media research of sites such as Facebook, Twitter, and Instagram, in which both the authors of the posts and the social media platforms have claims to ownership of the data. Large data management is continually evolving, requiring new data governance to address data ownership, security, privacy, and data sharing. For example, the transfer of location-based information over networks has raised privacy concerns for data owners (Sivarajah et al., 2017; Yi et al., 2014).

When researchers create big data projects, significant investments have been made to streamline processes, while privacy issues often hinder the sharing of data between organizations and between departments within large organizations (Krishnamurthy & Desouza, 2014). Much digital data is ubiquitous, continuously and naturally occurring, and publicly accessible. Despite being authored to fulfill a particular social function, it becomes analyzed and shared for an unintended purpose, with unintended effects from the perspective of the research participants (Lyon, 2001).

The public is becoming increasingly aware of these risks, which can lead to self-suppression and greater caution when sharing content in online spaces. The risks of sharing personal information online contribute to problems of erroneous content in media or online data (Trottier, 2014), and the need for researchers to distinguish between truth and fake news, and between fictitious and genuine online identities, and to ensure the reliability of research claims. User-generated web content is always "curated" by the author in some way to present a particular version of reality or fiction. Public awareness of privacy and security issues in online environments has begun to shape more cautious public engagement with digital technologies (Trottier, 2014).

Challenges of big data acquisition

A key issue for qualitative researchers, who are often based in universities, is the problem of big data acquisition. Does big data afford easy access to large amounts of useful data? Digital data generated daily are potentially very useful, having the advantage of being almost completely networked between multiple things and people (boyd & Crawford, 2011).

However, there are important questions to ask about who gets access to big data, under what terms, and for what purposes (Qiu, 2015). Complex research questions about human behavior and society require identification of patterns within relevant data, and these data are typically owned by individuals and organizations. Access may depend on a convergence of interests or goodwill from the owners of different data sources, and often the payment of large fees. The use of big data is similarly encumbered by established institutional protocols and issues of ownership, human relationships, and new implications for research ethics that are only beginning to be understood (Mills, 2017).

Despite the claims about the usefulness of big data that is put to secondary uses, and calls to make other (non-big) data accessible for secondary uses through open data, many qualitative research areas are data-poor fields where good data are hard-won and precious (Sawyer, 2008). Qualitative researchers are typically rewarded for generating original data, and few would disagree that competitive research funding is often awarded to those who are gathering something fresh, or who are analyzing data in new ways to solve complex problems using innovative techniques. Reusable data, whether repurposed big data, or open access smaller data, is becoming increasingly important in research of astronomy, social media, town modeling, public health, climate research, and dry lab research in the biosciences, to name a few fields (Borgman, 2015). Yet the most competitive grants and publications are those that address topics and provide solutions for problems that require new data, bigger quantities of data than in the past, or data collection, reduction, and analysis in more innovative and cost-efficient digital ways (Mills, 2017).

A sizable proportion of potentially repurposed big data will remain proprietary data. Certain data cannot be released by law—embargo periods may apply that delay the use of data beyond its period of relevance—and individual human research data may be too sensitive (Borgman, 2015). Entities that have the power to release data may see that the risks and the hidden costs necessary to make the data useable and interpretable outweigh the benefits of releasing data for use by others. Big data produced by companies or social media sites require vast amounts of attention to maintaining and organizing metadata to be able to reuse the data. Furthermore, big data rendered in digital form are potentially more short-lived than cultural artifacts and even paper records, due to the rapid change of technologies and the software used to store and analyze them. In addition, the further from its origin that data are extracted and applied, the further data are open to complex issues of ethics, access, and decontextualization (Mills, 2017).

Challenges of big data   29

Even in a context in which social media data has exploded, researchers who work for companies like Google, Facebook, or Microsoft will have vastly privileged access to data that university-based qualitative researchers do not. Typically, social media companies are the gatekeepers of very large social data, while corporate entities typically restrict access to data or charge a fee for researchers to access smaller data sets (Manovich, 2011). In their much-cited article, boyd and Crawford (2012, p. 22) argue that "those without access can neither reproduce nor evaluate methodological claims of those who have privileged access". Therefore, social media end users simply cannot access and process the same velocity of data as the internet giants (Trottier, 2014). Certain internet giants and researchers based in industrial roles have even suggested that academics are ill-equipped to research social media data that industry can do better, thus undermining the research community by designating insiders and outsiders (boyd & Crawford, 2012).

Researchers who have attempted to share big data have also demonstrated the difficulties that arise when making data available to other researchers in ethically responsible ways, such as by de-identifying the original data for use by other researchers. Daries and colleagues (2014) shared data generated from Massive Open Online Courses (MOOCs), with the twofold goal to permit other researchers to: (1) reproduce the outcomes of the analysis and (2) perform new analyses beyond the initial research. They were required to de-identify the data to protect student privacy under the district regulatory regime, but when they compared statistics on the original data set and the de-identified data, there were major discrepancies. For example, the original study found that 5 percent of the students enrolled had received certificates, while the curated data set cut that percentage by half (Mills, 2017). Such modifications distort the "truth" of the original data set considerably, because analysis of the modified data sets may result in incorrect statistics. For example, the information may be incomplete, particularly when anonymized, so that researchers cannot adjust for demographic factors, like age, gender, and socioeconomic factors. Scholars in some fields are uncertain about the utility of the open, reusable data for replication or innovative analysis by other researchers (Daries et al., 2014). This case illustrates the fundamental tension between generating and curating data sets that meet the ethics requirement of anonymity, while providing useful, openly accessible data to advance new knowledge (Mills, 2017).

Similarly, there are big data divides entangled with issues of access: Between those who have access to big data and those who do not, between those who have the computational expertise and means to analyze it and those who do not. There is a chasm between those who need essential community collections of big data to answer their questions and those who prefer to work longitudinally with a cultural community. Even when researchers have easier access to shared big data via national data repositories, there is the problem of misinterpretation and misuse. Social media data must be interpreted with an understanding that user-generated content is usually carefully curated, and is not a transparent window into the self (Labrinidis & Jagadish, 2012). Mayer-Schönberger and Cukier (2013) warn that underlying data used to generate knowledge may be big, but could be used inappropriately (Mills, 2017).

Big data, like small data, may be biased, misused, or misleading, and fail to capture what authorities or internet giants purport that it quantifies. However, when compared to the use of small data, the consequences of big data misuse will be much greater. And while big data has the potential for optimizing and advancing the efficiency of research and scholarship, more than ever before, there is the need for reason, theorization, problem-solving, originality, and social justice in determining what questions can be served by the data and whose interests they serve (Mills, 2017).

The ready supply of big data does not mean that rare data sets no longer exist or are no longer needed in many fields of research. There will always be the need for difficult-to-obtain qualitative data. A ready supply of statistics and the vast scale of data in the digital world are often not useful for answering the kinds of research questions that qualitative researchers are asking. For example, how can big data help us understand remote Indigenous communities and their cultural beliefs and epistemologies? How can we study rare chromosomal disorders through big data, since there are very few people in the world who have these conditions? While many rural contexts cannot escape from digital transformation, there are likely to be digital data research "black spots"—research about people who have limited access to the internet, such as those in remote rural areas, the very elderly, the very ill, the disabled, children, refugees, people living in infrastructure that has been destroyed by natural disasters, and babies too young to leave a digital footprint, to name a few examples (Mills, 2017).

Most importantly, the value of data is not tied to the data itself, but to what questions can be answered by those data. Even when researchers think they are asking valuable questions about data and publish the findings, millions of research articles that are openly accessible to the public on Google Scholar remain uncited by people beyond their own

Challenges of big data 31

research teams for years, raising questions about the cost of making raw data reusable to produce more uncited papers that are competing for attention in a data- and opinion-overloaded world. Creative use of big data requires being able to ask the significant questions within a research field at relevant times in history, while finding a fit between readily available data and the most pressing human problems to forge new frontiers of theory (Mills, 2017).

Challenges of BDA

A challenge of analyzing big data is to do so in a way that brings "Big Value" (Sivarajah et al., 2017). The next step after data acquisition is to extract the required information from the underlying sources and to translate it into a form suitable for analysis (Labrinidis & Jagadish, 2012). Even if data is acquired inexpensively, such as through open access databases, the purposeful use of big data is often very costly because the information collected will typically not be in a format ready for analysis. Labrinidis and Jagadish (2012) elaborate some of the difficulties of BDA:

> Data analysis is considerably more challenging than simply locating, identifying, understanding, and citing data. For effective large-scale analysis all of this has to happen in a completely automated manner. This requires differences in data structure and semantics to be expressed in forms that are computer understandable, and then robotically resolvable. Even for simpler analyses that depend on only one data set, there remains an important question of suitable database design.
> (p. 2032)

Large-scale data mining requires efficient accessibility, integration, and cleaning of trustworthy data, and suitable computing environments with interfaces that support declarative query and the use of scalable mining algorithms (Labrinidis & Jagadish, 2012).

BDA is now often performed by data scientists—dubbed the "sexiest" profession of the twenty-first century—while the current and predicted future shortage of highly skilled professional in this field is a commonly cited problem (Davenport & Patil, 2012). This has potential consequences for data analysis, but also for locating skillful peer reviewers among the scientific community.

Technologies for BDA are developing rapidly, while the human resources to leverage big data are lagging behind. Currently, much of the sorting of valuable data still requires differing degrees of manual human analysis (Sivarajah et al., 2017). The high costs of big data analysis are associated with staff wages and specialized data training, though some predict that effectively deployed BDA, machine learning, and artificial intelligence will gradually lower the threshold of human effort and its associated expenditure (Davenport & Dyché, 2013). Big data monitoring, such as social media analytics, requires specialized hardware, software (e.g. advanced big data analyzing technologies), analytic methods, and staffing, which offset the cost savings of using open access data sources (Sivarajah et al., 2017).

While qualitative researchers may not ever need to use petabytes or zettabytes of data to answer research questions, digital data sets, particularly those that use moving visual data, are potentially much larger than those in previous decades. The sheer volume and velocity of big data is a well-recognized challenge for BDA, including its heterogeneity and ubiquity, which makes retrieving, processing, integrating, and analyzing large-scale data difficult without novel approaches and data mining techniques (Barnaghi et al., 2013). But qualitative researchers are not insulated from the trend towards digital data sets that can accumulate in richness, detail and size very significantly over short periods of time, even when researching modest numbers of research participants.

Similarly, qualitative researchers increasingly work with structured and unstructured digital data sets that are characterized by greater variety, such as video and audio recordings, screen capture, game play clips, digital compositions and games created by participants, mobile data, and data captured by sensors in wearable technologies (e.g. Go Pro cameras, Smart watches). Qualitative researchers are using a wider range of observational and textual data, including participant blogs, e-books, e-literature, digital archives, web analytics from participant dashboards, augmented and virtual reality data, emails, text messaging, policy documents, transactional data, and participant-generated web content, social media posts and web logs. The increased variety of qualitative and descriptive data sets calls for new ways of managing, combining, reducing, coding, analyzing, de-identifying, interpreting, and gaining value from heterogenous data sets that provide "thicker" and more detailed descriptions about participants, cases, cultural communities, or design-based research interventions than ever before.

In the context of the digitization in society and across all fields of research, increasingly larger data sets are transforming the way qualitative researchers work. There are now examples of enormous, longitudinal, and cross-national narrative data sets, such as the HIV prevention study which was based on 2000 narratives sampled from a larger set of 75,000 narratives collected during 1997–2014 in South Africa (Winskell, Singleton, & Sabben, 2018). The large-scale research systematically compared contextualized, social, and cultural representations of HIV in countries with varied sociocultural, epidemiological, and policy history, without sacrificing narrative richness. The sampling, data management, and analysis strategies used in the study enabled the identification of patterns across the participating countries—Burkina Faso, Kenya, Nigeria, Senegal, and Swaziland and time points (1997, 2000, 2002, 2005, 2011, 2013, and 2014), and permitted the in-depth analysis of thematically linked groups of transcribed texts (many of the original texts were handwritten).

Research interest in storytelling, narrative inquiry, and similar qualitative research methods is growing (Winskell et al., 2018), with ever-increasing masses of descriptive data now able to be accumulated, managed, coded, and translated to quantitative formats to map the distributions, frequencies, and intersections of thematic codes to enable comparisons. Descriptive data analytics is the simplest form of big data that reveals what has already occurred (as opposed to predictive or prescriptive analytics) to identify, describe, and summarize patterns in dialogue, text, or observed social action that is analyzed after it has occurred (Sivarajah et al., 2017). If big and small data are seen as a continuum, rather than as a dichotomy, then qualitative researchers who have traditionally worked with small sample sizes may increasingly deal with larger and thicker digital data sets in a digital age. As narrative data thickens, there is a growing need for researchers to familiarize themselves with more automatized and efficient digital methods of descriptive data analytics.

4 Potentials of big data analytics for qualitative researchers

In the age of "petatides" or "zettafloods" of data, big data analytics has become a buzzword in the research literature, while larger digital data sets sometimes call for new methodologies, data collection methods, analytic tools, and theories to engage in data-intensive inquiry. This is occurring across a range of research fields, from the physical and social sciences (Hey, Tansley, & Tolle, 2009), to education (Smith, Cope, & Kalantzis, 2017), and to the arts and humanities (Borgman, 2009), sometimes referred to as "humanities 2.0" and "digital humanities" (Delyser & Sui, 2013). As human relationships and social action become mediated by digital technologies, qualitative methods are undergoing a gradual transformation, such as ethnographies in online environments that are now aptly called "netnographies" (O'Donohoe, 2010), employed by social media scholars to effectively research the social interactions of youth (Montgomery, 2015).

The growth of digital humanities is similarly associated with increased efforts to cross conventional qualitative-quantitative divides (Delyser & Sui, 2013). This chapter points to some of the potential synergies between qualitative approaches and big data analytics, as researchers work with larger and more heterogenous data sets and use computer-assisted analytic tools with increased affordances for mixed methods research designs. It explores some of the new techniques and directions for adapted methodologies for qualitative researchers to optimize hybrid analytics methods—text mining, opinion mining or sentiment analysis, data visualization, netnography, mobile research methods, follow-the-thing methods, and rhythmanalysis. It considers the use of multimodal analysis for heterogenous digital texts that combine images, words, audio, and other modes, and which span multiple media.

Text mining

Text mining and text analysis have recently gained the spotlight due to the rise of big data, becoming synonymous for a broad range of computational methods that search, retrieve, and analyze textual data. Text mining originated in information management fields, while text analysis began in the humanities with the manual analysis of text, such as indexing and alphabetical Biblical concordances. Text mining or text analytics seeks to extract relevant information from document collections, enabling the exploration of interesting patterns in unstructured document data (Truyens & Van Eecke, 2014).

Text mining involves applying a text mining tool to large collections of documents that contain written words, such as diverse collections of journal articles, social media posts, advertisements, or emails. Researchers can use it to quickly and efficiently locate relevant information to answer a research question, particularly in cases where the amount of textual data is very large. Rather than simply searching for key words, as occurs in a Google search, text mining searches for more precise concepts, phrases, sentences, and relationships, drawing on Natural Language Processing (NLP) algorithms, with techniques to examine words in their context, and to recognize similar concepts to draw inferences from the data.

The steps of text mining broadly involve gathering the text, preprocessing (data preparation and transformation), and then indexing terms to create a list of words, their location in the textual data, and numerical values, allowing structuring of the processed data. Next, mining of the preprocessed data involves identifying terms, disambiguating concepts, and identifying relationships between terms, including algorithm, inference, and information extraction. Finally, analysis of the raw results involves evaluation and data visualization to support interpretation in relation to the research questions under investigation.

While qualitative researchers typically do not have the expertise of computer scientists to conduct text mining, they may collaborate in research teams with text mining experts. Researchers can take introductory text mining courses within their disciplines to develop relevant skills, since this is no longer the exclusive domain of the computer sciences—particularly as text mining software becomes more common. Qualitative researchers collect descriptive and textual data that often requires some form of computer-assisted or semiautomatic text analysis. Computer-assisted text analysis uses a combination of statistical and pattern-based approaches to support qualitative research designs, and involves more than simply counting frequencies of words (Wiedemann, 2013). For example, open vocabulary analysis can permit multiword sequences to create semantic maps to show concept clusters and taxonomic relationships. NLP of this kind can optimize the richness of raw, qualitative data to efficiently identify themes (Wenzel & Van Quaquebeke, 2018). At the same time, "merely mining the data provides neither context, analysis, nor interpretation" (Delyser & Sui, 2013, p. 296). This is where synthesizing qualitative and quantitative forms of analysis may strengthen research designs or research reporting.

The use of data processing for large documents became associated with quantitative content analysis from the 1960s, influencing qualitative researchers' perceptions of text analysis software. For some decades, the idea of using computers for qualitative data analysis was viewed with skepticism because of a history of imperfect quantitative content analysis, and to avoid reductionist positivist epistemologies historically associated with such methods (see: Wiedemann, 2013). Additionally, qualitative researchers do not assume that it is always advantageous to increase the number of cases in a qualitative research design by using computer software, while potentially losing creativity, attention to individual stories, and unanticipated findings through human or manual coding (Kuckartz, 2007).

The use of computer software for qualitative analysts has been accepted only gradually since the late 1980s (Wiedemann, 2013). Some critique that most early forms of qualitative analysis software packages remained truly qualitative by simply replicating manual coding, organizing, and memo writing "formerly conducted with pens and highlighters, scissors, and glue" (Kuckartz, 2007, p. 16). In 1981, one of the first qualitative analysis programs, NUD*IST software, standing for Non-numerical Unstructured Data Indexing Searching and Theorizing was developed by Tom Richards, changing the way data was analyzed manually by qualitative researchers. In 1989, MAX was released for personal computer (DOS Windows), renamed in 2001 with an.rtf format. In 1999, QSR released NVivo, with a variety of software packages for qualitative coding becoming available around the same time, such as MAXQDA and later, ATLAS.ti and many others (Wiedemann, 2013).

Applying principles of genomics, new analytic strategies have been developed for text, which handle lexical items in a similar way as a cultural gene. Known as "culturomics" (e.g. http://www.culturomics.org/), within digital humanities, such forms of data mining afford new potentials for textual analytics (Michel et al., 2010). Culturomics and tools similar to

Google's Ngram database (https://books.google.com/ngrams), for example, may be utilized to address research problems, cultural trends, or disciplinary patterns, which were previously difficult to analyze qualitatively (Michel et al., 2010). Today, qualitative researches, who may not have previously considered using it, can now work with large text corpora, and search databases of digitalized artworks, images, newspapers, digital books, articles, or music. They can potentially find cultural and social patterns from millions of status updates, cell phone records, sensor data, and dashboard data. Much data is now digitally searchable, while quantitative data mining methods may have particular purchase in certain studies and fields (Berry, 2012; Bodenhamer, Corrigan, & Harris, 2010). The era of big data and digitally mediated research is opening up different kinds of fusions and interactions between qualitative and quantitative approaches, even if the "quantification" involves, at the most elementary level, translating textual data into frequencies, or creating visualizations of patterned words and themes (Borgman, 2009; Delyser & Sui, 2013; Sieber, Wellen, & Jin, 2011).

The realization of the text mining potentials for qualitative data analysis has only recently emerged (Wiedemann, 2016). Scholars in some fields have conducted studies that highlight the use of data or text mining strategies to analyze qualitative data, such as interviews in pediatric cancer patient research (Rasid, Nohuddin, Alias, Hamzah, & Nordin, 2017). Qualitative data mining (QDM) has been used in child welfare research to process unstructured and existing narrative data (e.g. risk assessments, investigative narratives, court reports, and contact notes) that are held in administrative data systems about children in foster care (Henry, Carnochan, & Austin, 2014).

For example, the research by Henry and colleagues (2014) first applied code-based data analysis to map the types of phenomena that were captured in the administrative database, followed by a "within case" analysis to describe individual cases. QDM often involves identifying bounded sites, contexts, or cases for analysis, and can be invaluable in fields where administrative documentation has proliferated and administrative data systems have made these data more accessible to researchers. Such collaborations require strong relationships of trust and shared interests between university and industry or agency partners, with secure data retrieval and protocols for maintaining confidentiality.

Wiedemann (2016) recently observed that debates about the use of software to analyze qualitative research have diminished, and computer-assisted qualitative data analysis (CAQDA) has been widely received (Wiedemann, 2013). CAQDA and computer-assisted mixed methods research analysis are increasingly used to manage very large qualitative and mixed methods data sets, with related software offering functionality to support an array of analytic methods, such as open coding, linking and organizing data, content analysis, transcription analysis, conversation analysis, discourse analysis, grounded coding, and recursive abstraction (Banner & Albarrran, 2009). However, qualitative researchers are conscious that the technologies or software for analysis is not ideologically benign, because its design and affordances play a role in how knowledge is shaped (Wiedemann, 2016).

Opinion mining or sentiment analysis

An area of big data analytics that has gained traction is sentiment analysis, emotion AI (artificial intelligence), or opinion mining, which is applied to research that aims to understand opinions or affect in large, unstructured textual environments (Ragini, Anand, & Bhaskar, 2018). The main task of sentiment analysis, a type of machine learning, is the detection, extraction, and quantification of subjective expression in textual data by classifying polarity of sentiment—positive or negative (Troisi, Grimaldi, Loia, & Maione, 2018). Some argue that neutral sentiment can or should also be important in certain analyses (Koppel & Schler, 2006). Sentiment analysis may also attend to discreet emotions, such as happiness, satisfaction, anger, and disgust (Shayaa et al., 2018). Advanced sentiment analysis may attend to numerical coding of the intensity, force, or graduation of the sentiment— how strong the sentiment is—which can be realized grammatically with intensified lexis (e.g. uneasy +1, anxious +2, petrified +3) and assigned mathematical values (El Alaoui et al., 2018).

Opinion mining and sentiment analysis are supported by the use of software to identify and classify opinion computationally, such as through NLP, text analysis, computational linguistics, and biometrics to determine the attitude of the writer (Banerjee, 2016). For example, Leximancer™ supports a form of automatic sentiment analysis, allowing researchers to select user-defined constructs, such as positive and negative sentiment. By simply clicking the positive or negative "sentiment lens" button, researchers can track favorability measures within text, based on an expansive thesaurus of affect terms and their derivatives (e.g. anger, angered, angering, and angers).

Qualitative researchers and applied linguists have developed frameworks for manually analyzing opinion or attitudes in discourse or written text, such as Martin and White's (2005) appraisal framework, which may potentially be extended to refine sentiment analysis techniques, software development, and for optimizing user-options in text mining software. Such analytic work (manual) has been extended to the multimodal analysis of affect in photographs (Mills, 2016), animations and audiovisual texts (Mills & Unsworth, 2018), and other multimodal texts that combine words, images, audio, and other modes to show opinion (Economou, 2009).

In conventional discourse analysis of affect, applied linguists can attend to comparative and superlative morphology (somewhat, quite, most), repetition (very, very pleased), and punctuation (exclamation marks). Manual coding can account for emoticons that are used in short digital text, and SMS language and chat abbreviations ("ILY" for "I love you") with meanings that are shifting much faster than other formal language.

Colloquialisms containing reverse sentiment may be misinterpreted without accounting for context in sentiment analysis of informal texts (e.g. sinful or wicked chocolate cake is positive). Expressions of assessment are based on modal auxiliaries (may, might, could, must), modal adjuncts (perhaps, probably, definitely) and modal attributes (possible, likely, unlikely) (Martin & White, 2005).

Online sentiment detection is complicated in machine learning—a set of methods to automatically detect patterns in data, and then to predict future data or perform other decision-making with certainty (Murphey, 2012). This is because forms of communication, such as text messaging, frequently include abbreviations, truncated sentences, and adaptations of grammar and spelling. However, this is an area that is rapidly developing, and researchers have now developed algorithms for machine learning, such as Sentistrength™, to address some of these issues. This program includes sentiment word strength lists, a training algorithm to optimize sentiment word strengths, spelling correction algorithms, booster word lists, negating word lists, repeated letters, exclamation marks, repeated punctuation, and ignoring of negative words used in questions (Thelwall, Buckley, Paltoglou, & Cai, 2010). However, the extent to which machine learning is able to match human ability to manually identify emotion manually in written text is still debated (Thelwall et al., 2010), and multimodal texts that include combinations of human emotive gestures, postures, facial expressions, music, and other modes add further complexity.

Even humans disagree on sentiment in language, bringing different sociocultural, linguistic, and psychological factors to the analysis of feelings—evaluating sentiment is not an exact science. Understanding the meaning and function of emotion terms cannot be analyzed by frequencies, but by lexico-grammar patterns and context (Bednarek, 2015). At the same time, with the proliferation of online texts that indicate sentiment through reviews, ratings, emoticons, and "like" buttons, the unstructured data of online opinion has become a form of virtual and political currency. The analysis of online opinion can be supported by qualitative and quantitative principles and algorithms for sentiment analysis, necessary for the meaningful interpretation and theorization of emotive textual data.

Information and data visualization

Information and data visualization are often referenced in big data research because there are new complexities for the interpretation and presentation of big data analytics. Large data needs to be communicated to others in ways that are easily grasped, and which leads to action or impact (Tay et al., 2017). At the same time, an array of new big data visualization techniques and software abound for making sense of data and its relations, primarily for the purpose of data exploration.

As early as the 1970s, researchers promoted the use of visualization to explore raw data as a critical first step in research, which can enable researchers to see data in a new light, often revealing the unexpected (Kirk, 2012). Visualization can also be very useful for displaying data at the end of a research project. Visualization can be applied to both quantitative and qualitative data. While many are familiar with Wordle and tag clouds, there are multiple visualization formats, from two-dimensional or planer (including geospatial) and three-dimensional (volumetric), network, temporal, multidimensional, and hierarchical. Visual forms of representation have become a credible approach to qualitative data analysis and presentation, supported by the expansion of new tools and software.

Very few qualitative studies aim to visualize narrative data from interviews, yet recent research has demonstrated that this is useful and very possible. Research designs that combine multiple forms of digital data and analytic processes are becoming more common, such as social media language analysis in organizational studies, where researchers can bring together the qualitative and quantitative data analysis in the same paper, visually encoding both dimensions of information content and frequency.

For example, Pokorny and colleagues (2016) developed a way to create network graphs from codes that were applied to qualitative transcripts using code names and their chronological location. The approach enabled the quantification of the qualitative codes using network analysis and graph theory, which is particularly suitable for examining interrelations among the codes. They were then able to relate associations of network indices with other quantitative variables using common statistical procedures. Bazeley (2010) has similarly demonstrated the transformation of qualitative coding into numerical values for statistical analysis, with results presented as visual displays of relationships.

Another current example of the novel application of data visualization for qualitative research has been led by multimodal semiotics. For example, the multimodal mixed methods research framework by O'Halloran and colleagues (2018) is based on computational methods for multimodal discourse analysis. In mixed methods research designs, qualitative and quantitative data often remain as distinct data sets, despite aiming for their meaningful integration (Guetterman, Fetters, & Creswell, 2015). The multimodal framework extends advanced mixed methods research that draws on data mining and information visualization for big data analytics. It enables the interactive and visual representation of abstract data, extending data merging that involves standard statistical techniques, graphs, and text-based information displays (for in-depth description, see: O'Halloran et al., [2018]).

O'Halloran and colleagues (2018) contend, "[b]uilding on theory from information design, computer graphics, human-computer interaction, and cognitive science...information visualization permits researchers to explore patterns in large, multidimensional data sets in new ways" (p. 28). Such visualizations can enable the sharing of qualitative data in novel ways to generate original insights, while providing greater opportunities to combine and compare quantitative and qualitative results in mixed methods research. In particular, network visualizations are highly effective when they integrate both numerical and textual data, enabling researchers to ask new questions about the data (Tay et al., 2017).

Netnography

Netnography is an ethnographic approach to social media research that has the potential to integrate big data analytic methods, while upholding similar principles and methods as qualitative research, ethnography, critical ethnography, and action research. Netnography begins with the view that the unadapted application of usual qualitative research methods to online contexts, such as ethnography and participant observation, can be problematic, since these methodologies were originally intended for face-to-face contexts (Caliandro, 2014). There is now a growing range of digital methods that are particularly well suited to research using big data and digital environments, such as those that involve participant crowdsourcing of data collection (Marciano, Allen, Hou, & Lach, 2013), and social network analysis (Pokorny et al., 2016; Tay et al., 2017). Some netnographers constrain their data sets to small data, and apply qualitative analytic tools, such as discourse analysis (Cheek, 2004). Other netnographic researchers incorporate large online and unstructured data, integrating computational analyses and visualization methods. These netnographers are united by the use of data sets that largely originate in, or manifest through, internet and mobile data, akin to participant-observational data, but often collected remotely from the participants (Kozinets, 2015). In many netnographic research designs, this data is often supplemented by other digital data, such as emails, recorded video calls, and many other digital and face-to-face methods. Online content may be comprised of textual data, photographs, graphics, music, video, and other formats, depending on the purpose of the research.

An array of ethnographic approaches has been described to account for ethnography in online environments, including digital ethnography (Murthy, 2008), netnography (Caliandro, 2014; Kozinets, 2015), virtual ethnography (Hine, 2000), web ethnography (Puri, 2007), smartphone ethnography (Melles, 2004), and mobile ethnography (Büscher & Urry, 2009). These qualitative approaches have emerged as more than a set of fashionable neologisms for arbitrary variations of ethnographic methodology. Rather, these approaches attempt to address fundamental and different logistical challenges of human research that are mediated by digital relations.

Recent forms of netnography, such as the approach in Kozinets' (2015) volume, remain grounded in essential ethnographic approaches, such as participant observation, while seeking to broaden the scope of qualitative research. More recent adaptations of qualitative methods include videography, social network analysis, social media research presence, visualization methods, and selective forms of data science and analytics. Netnography is very suitable to complement social network analysis, big data analytics, smart data, surveys, and predictive modeling. Similarly, digital netnographies often draw on the use of computational techniques from big data analytics, including social network analysis. Intelligent adaptation of older methodologies, rather than discarding conventional qualitative approaches, is becoming more common (Kozinets, 2015). Thus, in a big data era, qualitative researchers can look to a widening range of qualitative approaches to online research, such as digital ethnography (Lohmeier, 2014), netnography (O'Donohoe, 2010), and social media ethnography (Postill & Pink, 2012).

Follow-the-thing methods

Follow-the-thing methods may hold new potentials in a big data era (Delyser & Sui, 2013), with the rise of the Internet of Things (IoT)—the interconnected internet of everyday devices that can send and receive data (Adams, 2017). Follow-the-thing ethnographic methods trace the journey of material things for knowledge purposes, such as the route from production to consumption in capitalist societies, while documenting their cultural meanings, function, and associated practices (Delyser & Sui, 2013). The digital connection of sensor and other data from the IoT affords new potentials for tracking the everyday life of objects.

The increasing interconnectedness of things is exemplified in the use of radio frequency identification (RFID) tags—implanted microchips that are as small as a grain of rice, and embedded in clothing, toys, pets, products, credit cards, and passports (Hayles, 2009; Mills, 2017), as well as global information systems, mobile devices, sensors, and associated digital tracking technologies.

To illustrate, Bluetooth tracking device or GPS trackers, such as TrackR Pixel™ and Tilemate™, are increasingly purchased and attached to car keys, wallets, handbags, and other portable, personal items to locate them when misplaced or lost. Many digital devices have built-in, location-based services to approximate the location of a mobile phone and its owner, used by telecommunications companies, users, and family members via location sharing apps. Public transport services often require the use of cards that digitally trace passenger journeys and the associated use of credit. It is becoming easier with each new technological development to track the material life of things.

Follow-the-thing methods emerged as early as mid-1990s in the context of discussion of multisite ethnography (Marcus, 1995), drawing on theories of the famous work, the Social Life of Things, by Appadurai (1986). For example, Lash and Lury (2007) follow the movement of cultural objects and brands, including Toy Story™, Wallace and Gromit™ short feature films, Nike™, Swatch™, Trainspotting™, Euro '96™, and young British artists (YBA™), as they move through transformations across countries. Others have mapped the trajectories and reuse of shipping materials (Gregson, Crang, Ahamed, Akhter, & Ferdous, 2010). Hui (2012) applied follow-the-thing methods involving qualitative research methods to follow the socio-material life of things involved with bird watching and patchwork quilting. Centering on the tangible, inanimate objects within these social practices, the research showed how the transit of objects creates new opportunities for their use, such as in multisite performances and instances of consumption on the move. The emergence of the geospatial web has opened up affordances for tracking the location of objects in follow-the-thing methods. Mills and Comber (2015) have elaborated on socio-spatial and socio-material research trends more broadly:

> Geospatial tools have emerged via the Geoweb, such as the widely accessible Google Maps and Google Earth platforms, and other competing developments…there are new challenges for sociospatial literacy researchers to explore new forms of geospatial data collection, analysis, and reporting, incorporating moving visual images, network analysis, and other spatial presentations of data.
> (p. 100)

The geospatial web describes the merging of location-based information with information accessed on the internet (Mitchell, 2018). With the rise of geospatial tracking and monitoring of devices, objects, and users, Delyser and Sui (2013, p. 289) argue that geospatial mapping of the mobilities of things will become possible for longitudinal research, having "profound implications for human-geographic research", particularly for understanding mobile things and people. At that same time, they warn that such transformations trigger new "ethical concerns for the people whose lives these things touch and thereby monitor" (p. 298).

Mobile research methods

Another area of research that holds potential for qualitative researchers to make connections with big data are mobile research methods (Delyser & Sui, 2013). Mobile research methods examine mobilities of things or people, whether virtual or real, digital or non-digital, which can be conducted remotely or with research participants on the move (D'Andrea, Ciolfi, & Gray, 2011; Delyser & Sui, 2013). A reinvigoration of mobile methods is enabled by the expansion of global mobilities, mobile telecommunication, the geoweb, wearable technologies, and the ubiquity of mobile communication practices and location-based data services. Cultural geographers, sensory ethnographers, multimodal semioticians, interdisciplinary researchers, and others have demonstrated novel and significant research applications involving participants "on the go".

Using sensory ethnography as a collaborative methodology, Sunderland, Bristed, Gudes, Boddy and Da Silva (2012) investigated social determinants of health in place by walking, talking, and filming with community participants. The study used a variety of methodologies, including go-along interviews with key informants, participant observation, and casual conversation with locals on buses, documentary photography, sensory walks, and filmed street interviews. Many of the methods enabled the research team to capture insider perspectives on the go. In related research, Mills, Unsworth, Bellocchi, Park, and Ritchie (2014) conducted sensory ethnography with elementary school children to understand children's emotions in the materiality of lived, embodied, and situated experience of their local places. The children represented those sensorial experiences multimodally and viscerally through walking with the camera.

In another example, multimodal semioticians (Jaworski & Thurlow, 2017) explored non-verbal communication involving gesture and movement (kinesics) in tourist spaces through an analysis of video data captured as participant-tourist observer through the La Piazza del Duomo. Mobile research can utilize a wide range of old and new qualitative methods for data collection in transit, from handwritten field notes and walking interviews, to walking with video, dash cameras, action cameras (e.g. GoPro™), and other wearable and mobile recording devices, or alternatively, using crowdsourced and distributed research methods to capture research from a distance (Bancroft, Karels, Murray, & Zimpfer, 2014).

Mobile research methods are sometimes seen as a part of a "mobilities turn" towards theorizing space in dynamic ways across a range of disciplines, positioning mobilities at the nucleus of social relations (Grieco & Urry, 2016). In societies in which flows of big data, information, objects, and ideas are speeding up, including virtual and imagined mobilities, there is good reason to "adopt less static methods of exploring our mobile social worlds" (Murray, 2009, p. 1).

Multimodal analysis

Multimodal analysis is a potential space for the analysis of large and heterogenous, digital data sets that incorporate combinations of images, words, audio, gestures, textures, and other modes across multiple media. The term multimodality refers to the constitution of multiple modes in semiosis or meaning making (Bezemer & Kress, 2014). Modes are defined differently across schools of thought, and the classification of modes is somewhat contested. However, from a social semiotic approach, modes are the socially and culturally shaped resources or semiotic structures for making meaning (Jewitt, 2017). Specific examples of modes from a social semiotic perspective include speech, gesture, written language, music, mathematical notation, drawings, photographic images, or moving digital images (Mills & Unsworth, 2017).

Data has long been multimodal, because human interaction involves diverse kinds of meanings, whether of spoken or written words, visual images, gestures, posture, movement, sound, or silence. Yet in recent decades, the affordances of people-driven digital media and online textual production have given rise to an exponential increase in the circulation of multimodal data in networked digital environments. Multimodal data production has become a taken-for-granted part of everyday life for many people, and across cultures and societies. There is now an ease of producing and working with digital data, images, music, video games, apps, and other media via the internet and mobile technologies (Mills & Unsworth, 2017). The big data era is an historical moment that is awash with possibilities for expanding the analysis of textual data to attend to the production and circulation of digital images, sounds, and other multimodal textual data that proliferate on the internet, and which are displayed on tablets, smart phones, and wearable technologies.

Rythmanalysis

Big data is produced by some central sources—media and social media, cloud platforms, the web, IoT, and data bases—that fundamentally emerge from social practices. These provide digital traces of human rhythms that may be characterized by continuity and disjuncture, flows, and fluxes, across multiple networks of globalized interaction, and from smaller to larger scales of interaction.

An approach that has new potentials to glean insights from big data sources is rhythmanalysis—the study of spatiotemporal rhythms and dynamic time-spaces—an approach that has continued to gain popularity (Delyser & Sui, 2013). Rhythms were first conceived by Lefebvre (2004, p. 8) as perceptible across a range of context and levels, related to the human body or a text or to events and institutions. Rhythms can become an analytic tool to understand the patterning of human experience in everyday life across places and time (Edensor, 2016a), and can be analyzed at an urban, regional, rural, state, national, or global level (Delyser & Sui, 2013). Rhythmanalysis, according to Edensor (2016a), leads to a recognition that "places are always in a process of becoming, seething with emergent properties, but usually stabilized by regular patterns of flow that possess particular rhythmic qualities whether steady or intermittent, volatile or surging" (p. 3).

Places are constituted by multiple networks, flows, and connections among objects, people, and data, which are characterized by rhythms, many of which offer ontological security and consistency for individuals and societies, with the ever-present possibility of rupture (Appadurai, 1990). For example, cities are characterized by flows and rhythms of people, commuter patterns, work schedules, retail activities, restaurant surges, waiting times, delivery schedules, electricity, water, money, social and weather patterns, telecommunication patterns, security and internet activities, and much more (Edensor, 2016a; Elliotte & Urry, 2010). As Edensor (2016b) argues, "the spatial scale through which rhythms resound needs to be accounted for"... such as "how national and global rhythms increasingly pulse through place" (p. 3). Data that are expanding in volume, velocity, variety, and value are now collected about these everyday urban rhythms, creating a history of their interconnections with other cities and nations around the globe.

Researchers in cultural, human, physical, and spatial geography have long explored the rhythms of society and the natural world, and of bodies and movement, with the intent to expand repertoires of research methods and methodologies (Edensor, 2016b). Rhythmanalysis can bring together hybrid qualitative and quantitative research of big data traces to analyze spatiotemporal patterns and tensions to interpret the role of spatiotemporal rhythms in the production of social space (Delyser & Sui, 2013). As Lefebvre (2004, p. 15) observed, "[e]verywhere where there is interaction between a place, a time, and an expenditure of energy, there is rhythm". Today there are steady streams of data that trace everyday rhythms, bringing opportunities to ask different questions about these patterns and their dynamic spatiotemporal specificities, and to potentially collect and analyze rhythmic data more rapidly, continuously, and in ways that can generate insight about the interconnectedness and disjunctures among rhythms.

Conclusion

This chapter has sought to illustrate a range of potential touch-points for qualitative researchers to engage with augmented, digital forms of qualitative methodologies in digital worlds, such as netnography and mobile research methods. It has envisioned the natural extension of CAQDA, rhythmanalysis, and multimodal analysis, and expanded repertoires of analytic processes and techniques for text and opinion mining, data visualization, and processing of image and audiovisual data that are now associated with the growing body of big data research.

The range of methodologies and methods outlined here for developing a synergistic relationship between big data analytics and qualitative forms of dealing with narrative, digital, unstructured data is by no means intended to be all-encompassing. Rather, it is a sampler of the diversified options that have arisen in the big data research and literature to date. Many of these connections are well-recognized, such as netnography, mobile research methods, and CAQDA, while others are still embryonic. At the same time, qualitative research is not diminishing, but rather, as simple Google Ngram search of the phrase "qualitative research" suggests, it continues to have a strong, upward trend in the literature.

While new opportunities for research innovation and new methods are opening up for researchers of digital data, both qualitative and quantitative, it is worth acknowledging that digital technologies embody particular social norms and values that are tied to who designs them, where they were designed, and why, including the institutional needs that they serve. When used uncritically, digital tools can serve to reinforce rather than challenge existing ideologies, power dynamics, and social inequities in ways that are uncritical. Similarly, the development of expertise, technologies, and other research infrastructure for big data analytics is unevenly distributed across disciplines and across the globe (Graham, Hale, & Stephens, 2011). Thus, researchers can be mindful of potential conflicts and inequities in terms of big data developments, including who gets to play a role in determining the direction of big data analytics, along with its associated social and technical apparatus (Burns, 2015). Researchers can adopt and adapt new practices critically, while recognizing the need to actively play a part in determining the future direction of the integration of big data in contemporary research environments.

5 Big data ethics, privacy, and dataveillance

The use of repurposed big data is fundamentally complicated by new concerns for ethics, privacy, and social equity. Social theorists since the 1990s have recognized the rising threat of manufactured risks—as opposed to external risks, such as natural disasters—including those brought about by digital and technological rationalization (see: Giddens, 1999). Yet the rise of big data has increased the scale of privacy risks to become one of the most significant human-made threats to societies' own making in the twenty-first century (Mills, 2017). The production of big data has become one of the "hazards and insecurities induced and introduced by modernization itself" (Beck, 1992, p. 21). While issues of privacy and data ownership were discussed in Chapter 3 (this volume), in relation to access and logistical problems for big data researchers, the current chapter looks at issues of consent, privacy, and dataveillance from an ethical perspective.

All data generation and analysis is inescapably tied to ethical concerns, but technological shifts in the production, sharing, and connectivity of big data from multiple sources creates new complexities for researchers who wish to reuse "naturally occurring" big data for research purposes. For example, some social media researchers analyze social network data collected by companies, while others critique the ethics of organizations that are permitted to collect such data about individuals (Borgman, 2015; Bruckman, Luther, & Fiesler, 2015). Additionally, risks to privacy have taken center stage in the context of the heightened invasiveness of many kinds of big data analysis. For instance, analysis with combined data sets based on geographic location and internet-based sources has been identified as potentially intrusive, even when such data are supposedly anonymous (Fuller, 2017). Regrettably, data are not always used in empowering or emancipatory ways for research participants, and in social contexts beyond academic purposes. Data are always generated for multiple social purposes including to leverage profits, track web usage, create user profiles, and generate predictive analytics, whether to manage an organization, forecast consumer behavior, or govern societies (Kitchin, 2014; Mills, 2017).

Privacy and dataveillance

Where previously a public-private dichotomy was characterized by physical privacy, such as determining the boundaries of one's home or personal property, this dichotomy is not paralleled in the world of informational privacy (Mai, 2016). Rather, as Daries et al. (2014) contends, "[i]n a contemporary networked digital information society people sit in their private homes connected to a public network, communicating with private friends using public wires, exchanging private information stored on public servers". In a big data society, the distinction between public and private has increasingly become blurred.

In a big data age, almost everyone reveals private and personal information either wittingly or unwittingly in the performance of everyday life—exchanging emails, downloading e-books and music, filling the car with petrol, reading the news, sharing photos, tagging friends, "liking" posts, buying milk, purchasing online, paying bills, and using a mobile phone (Allen, 2013). Irrespective of the reasons for revealing information, Mai (2016) contends: "[i]t is almost impossible to perform most daily activities without revealing personal information and providing fodder for data brokers and big data organizations, whether they are private or public" (pp. 192–193). It is standard and regulated practice to gain informed, written, and understood consent from anyone whose data is harvested. Therefore, many internet-based service providers who collect big data gain user consent through a "tick-the-box" form of agreement or consent. However, such agreements are typically oriented towards reducing risks and liabilities for those who are harvesting the data, with impracticably complex and lengthy terms and conditions that serve to obscure the participants' visibility over the use of their data (Fuller, 2017). As Wilbanks (2014, p. 235) has noted, internet service providers regularly attempt to minimize the ability of the data sharer "to comprehend the scope of data, and its usage, through a mixture of sharp design and obscure legal jargon".

Researchers have observed that the rapid amassing of big data has fast outpaced technological and legislative protection of individual privacy (Adams, 2017). For instance, there are frequent accounts in the news of high-profile data breaches and identity theft, particularly for businesses, where individual or personal data is exposed to unauthorized access that can result in loss of a financial, proprietary, reputational, or informational nature (Adams, 2017; Sen & Borle, 2015). Are those who consent to share their data with an organization made aware of such potential risks to their privacy? Users of digital technologies need to understand the way in which their data is generated and shared across devices and platforms, and with third parties, as well as be informed of the security risks in the event of a data breach. Protecting individual privacy in a big data era demands an approach to data analysis that prioritizes control of the data by the owner (Adams, 2017).

Some argue that detailed profiles of individuals can be generated from users' digital footprints—a phenomenon called dataveillance (Fuller, 2017; Raley, 2013). While the use of such monitoring data is useful for security services and official agencies to protect individuals from harm (e.g. security risks, unlawful activity), dataveillance can also become an infringement of privacy. The *Investigatory Powers Act 2016* (UK Parliament, c. 25), sometimes critiqued as the "snooper's charter", is an example of such uses, requiring web and phone companies to store web browsing histories for 12 months, and affording unprecedented access to the police, security services, and other government agencies (Fuller, 2017).

In many ways, the traditional "Data-Information-Knowledge-Wisdom" (DIKW) pyramid has fragmented, because data were formerly treated as isolated symbols without meaning, whereas information was seen as processed data that have gained meaning (see, e.g., Bellinger, Castro, & Mills, 2004). Big data are able to be rapidly processed and analyzed for correlations and patterns. Some argue that this process of datafication makes no distinction between data and information, for example, as every word in each book becomes searchable in databases like Google's Ngram Viewer (Mai, 2016). Indeed, some predict that datafication might potentially incorporate everything because most digital devices are networked, and daily activities of individuals and societies are digitally mediated (Mayer-Schönberger & Cukier, 2013).

Amplification of these risks to individual privacy are sometimes associated with the Internet of Things (IoT), because the IoT enables digital devices of many kinds to connect with local and virtual networks, communicating automatically with other devices, while continuously generating data (Borgohain, Kuman, & Sanyal, 2015). For example, smartphones are equipped with location-based sensors, generating real-time data about human time-space paths (Rghioui, Aziza, Elouaai, & Bouhorma, 2015). Even in countries where technologies are less accessible, mobile telecommunications services have expanded, as marketers use a plethora of applications that draw on global information systems (GIS) services to inform and enhance the capabilities of the user experience and the functionality of the device (Hayes, 2014, p. 50). Sensors are used in cars, home electronic devices, health monitoring equipment, smartphones, and smartwatches—a market with extensive economic value. These synchronized sensors enable users to check the status of certain home appliances, security and lighting systems, employee usage of work facilities, and so on, from smartphones or other networked dashboards and entities (Adams, 2017). Adams (2017) observes that "[t]aken together, the information from disparate devices provide extensive information on individual and behavioural patterns, which is a privacy concern".

Similarly, the continuous monitoring and surveillance of populations through the transmission of personal and product data can now be assisted by the use of radio frequency identification (RDIF) tags that are implanted microchips in products, passports, and many other things (Hayles, 2009). Constituting a kind of uberveillance or physical body monitoring, these technologies have even been used subdermally in pets, and have been approved for use in humans by the US Food and Drug Administration (Michael & Michael, 2014).

Consumers, products, and tangible things in built and digitally networked environments become linked "nodes in a web of algorithms" (Hayes, 2014, p. 50). This data is typically not collected to generate new knowledge, but to profit economically from daily social interaction (Mills, 2017; Rust, 2017). Other data technologies that have implications for privacy include Smartcards, national identification schemes, and genetic testing with its potential for discrimination. Related technologies include biometric imaging data such as facial scanning, retina scans, fingerprinting techniques, voice recognition, hand geometry, digital imagery, and DNA sampling (Crompton, 2002; Mills, 2017).

When it comes to property rights in internet research, there are complexities, because rights in the data may belong to the research participants, the internet companies or the researcher, or be shared among several owners. In addition, the power of internet companies to provide access to customer data, or to release data, varies by country and jurisdiction. Because of these property rights issues, many researchers prefer to generate and collect their own digital data directly from participants (Borgman, 2015).

Consent

Conventionally, research ethical clearance requires that researchers gain signed, informed consent, which typically does not include consent to any further investigation that may result from sharing, combining, or repurposing data. Similarly, data that are produced in public, such as social media data (e.g. tweets, posts, blogs), are not freely available to researchers without consent under most human research ethics guidelines (Borgman, 2015).

A strength of big data is the potential to reveal unforeseen connections, yet, at the same time, this potentially creates a problem for users who may be unaware of how digital data collected by internet companies will be shared with third parties who may mine the data for other purposes (Milton, 2017, p. 301). The trans-contextual nature of social media platforms, such as Facebook, means that information that was uploaded for a specific purpose can be repurposed without the user's awareness or consent, contributing to the normalization of "function creep"—when information authored for a specific purpose becomes recontextualized, or even decontextualized, in multiple and unintended future scenarios (Andrejevic, 2013; Lyon, 2001; Trottier, 2014).

Additionally, it is well recognized in big data research that small pieces of seemingly innocuous or disparate data can speak profoundly when combined, potentially exposing what were intended to be anonymous persons, rendering them visible (Milton, 2017). Risks are often increased in contexts of long-term data storage, where the greater passage of time results in data usage that is further removed from the original purposes, contexts, and terms of the consent. Furthermore, it is often not possible for researchers to make accurate judgments about the relative costs and benefits to the research subjects of their consent to reveal certain data. A consequence is that participants may consent to the use and disclosure of data when it is not in their best interests (Fuller, 2017; Solove, 2013). Additionally, questions often arise about the ownership of data, such as in the case of internet providers who are held accountable for the data use, and for those who use and share their personal data with internet services (Milton, 2017).

Another potential problem with consent in big data research is illustrated in research by Daries (2014), which involved the de-identification and sharing of data from MOOCs (Massive Open Online Courses) for secondary analysis. The researchers conducted a case study in de-identification using the k-anonymity approach, finding that the resultant curated data set for reuse was markedly different to the original data. Data possessing the k-anonymity property means that a set of quasi-identifying information for each participant cannot be distinguished from at least k-1 individuals whose data is similarly included in the data release, where k is the minimum number of subjects within the data set who share each set of potentially identifying characteristics

(Sweeney, 2002). The process of ensuring that the linked data met the k-anonymity requirement left the authors with conflicting results from their secondary data analysis. Thus, it appeared that compulsory regulatory requirements to anonymize data for repurposing by others can sometimes be incommensurate with the goals of scientific research. Resolving such incompatibilities will require new approaches that better balance the protection of privacy with the advancement of science in educational research and the social sciences more broadly (Daries et al., 2014).

Such findings are aligned to the concerns of big data theorists regarding problems with the anonymization or de-identification of big data when analytics involves triangulation between multiple data sets. For instance, some argue that linking a postal code and birthdate reduces the chances of identifying an individual to 1 in 80, while further linking gender and year of birth is sufficient to identify an individual (Koonin, Steven, & Holland, 2014). This has led to the view that anonymization is not a sufficient means of protecting privacy in some studies (Raley, 2013), while others assert that privacy and big data are incompatible (Barocas & Nissenbaum, 2014).

Some argue that the consent approach to privacy has ceased to be meaningful in the contemporary networked information society, because it relies on the assumption that individuals "make conscious, rational and autonomous choices about the processing of their personal data" (Schermer, Custer, & Van Der Hof, 2014, p. 171). Often, the issues involved in the release of data go beyond the limits of the individual "to make conscious decisions about their informational-self" (Mai, 2016, p. 196). The ability of rational individuals to limit or control information about themselves is impractical in datafied Western societies, while failing to take into account the power structures that work against individual choice. A key point to note is that a significant proportion of the information about individuals is not directly provided by anyone, but can be generated through predictive analytics (Mai, 2016; Solove, 2013).

Implications

Ethical issues in a big data age, whether online or offline, involve respect for research participants, whether the data is aggregated or not. In addition, there are regulations and guidelines about what data can be collected about people under what circumstances, and this can vary by country, state, jurisdiction, funding agency, and field, among other factors (Borgman, 2015). However, qualitative researchers can avoid ethical pitfalls when negotiating big data analysis by asking some key guiding questions (Dekas & McCune, 2015):

1. Is the research a normal part of operation for the participants, presenting no personal risks?
2. Are the participants very comfortable in their particular community with the use of data analytics?
3. Is there trust between participants and the researcher that the researcher and any collaborating organization has their best interests at heart?
4. Can participants be sure that the proposed analytic processes are unbiased?
5. Would the participants feel any hint of violation if they learned about the study findings and conclusions?

Any research is ethically unjustified if it exposes participants to significant risks in the pursuit of knowledge (Milton, 2017). For research to meet ethical requirements, there needs to be reasonable surety that the research will contribute valuable new knowledge, and that the involvement of human participants is necessary. In addition, there must be a favorable ratio of benefits over risks to the research participants, and appropriate strategies to protect privacy and confidentiality (Beauchamp & Childress, 2013). If such criteria are met, then potential participants can be invited to provide consent that is voluntary, informed, written and understood (Milton, 2017).

Qualitative researchers need to engage in critical practice to relocate and readdress the operation of big data, seeking to protect the privacy of self and others in research (Mills, 2017). Foucault's (1997, p. 44) useful points of critique can be applied to the ethical use of data to establish: "…how not to be governed like that, by that, in the name of those principles, with such and such an objective in mind, and by means of such procedures, not like that, not for that, not by them".

In contrast to secondary repurposing of big data, new big data may be generated from research-purposed technologies, such as distributing smart phones to participants or using sensors in specific research conditions to collect only data that is generated for the purposes and time period of the research. In each situation, researchers should critically evaluate the use of analytic procedures that might cause discomfort to the participants, or that are not in the best interests of the participants. Analytic procedures should be done in such a way that the findings can be trusted by the participants. These are the decisive ethical benchmarks (Bassett, 2015; Mills, 2017).

Conclusion

Big data researchers sometimes frame data analytics as a resource that is essentially untapped, and that is available to be "mined" or "harvested" like oil or grain (Trottier, 2014). Data becomes regarded as an incidental "by-product" of social interaction (Beer, 2012), like extracting molasses in the process of refining sugar. Such discourses require critical evaluation because "big data do not exist in a social vacuum. Their impact cannot be fully understood in the context of newly assembled configurations or 'game changing' discourses" (Trottier, 2014, p. 69). It is similarly vital to regard individuals as more than passive recipients of technology, but as knowing agents. Likewise, it is important to acknowledge the limitations of big data and its seemingly ubiquitous reach, conceding that there are also contexts of exclusion and unevenness in the populations that are accessible via big data, given the reality of social and digital divides (boyd & Crawford, 2012).

What is right or wrong use of data in research varies across times, cultures, and contexts, and research ethics are precipitously changing as data mining evolves. Likewise, views on privacy, anonymity, and consent are markedly changing and sometimes contentious (Borgman, 2015). Data that were previously private are no longer protected, due to the digital capabilities and interests of corporations through dataveillance, digital footprints, online profiles, corporate governance and other data-driven decision-making (Kitchin, 2014). No data generation and analysis can be free from complex ethical concerns, but the technological changes to the production, sharing, and repurposing of data raise new issues and pitfalls for social scientists who wish to harness big data for their scholarly purposes (Mills, 2017).

6 Anticipating big data futures for qualitative researchers

While researchers figure out how to access the right big data, big data is quickly accessing us. Predictive analytics mediate our online searches for goods and services, showing us what we should like, where we can find it nearby, and what others like us bought (Hand, 2014). Thrift (2005) reflects, "The materials of cyberspace are now infrastructural and anticipatory, knowing where to find us". What does the big data trend mean for qualitative research now and into the future? Smith (2014, pp. 184–185) states:

> The fate of qualitative research in this moment is…uncertain, and how qualitative research will contribute to and contest the "big data" challenge poses many questions.

While "big data" in the practical sense of the term pertains to structured and unstructured data sets that are typically too enormous for a single qualitative researcher to wrangle, the term big data is also a "meme", a "marketing term", and a "movement" (Lohr, 2012, para. 7; Parks, 2014, p. 355). In other words, the paradigmatic sense of the phenomenon, with its ideological assumptions about what counts as evidence for claims, is already shaping expectations about what research should be funded, and which kinds of research are more competitive and cutting edge (Bisel, Barge, Sougherty, Lucas, & Tracy, 2014). For this reason, there is some impetus for researchers of all methodological persuasions to know their own stance on big data. At the same time, researchers do not need to embrace epistemic assumptions that "big" or even "biggish" is better, especially given that most categories generated in qualitative research designs do not require millions of Tweets, posts, or other pieces of evidence to reach theoretical saturation.

Interestingly, big qualitative data researchers have suggested modified descriptors of the features of big data. Such defining criteria include

(a) high volume of textual or visual data, (b) highly complex data involving multiple points of triangulation, or (c) complex data analyses that provide unusually deep insights (Bisel et al., 2014; Hand, 2014). In many respects, the criteria are similar to general definitions of big data, with an emphasis on depth rather than breadth, acknowledging that qualitative data has a different kind of complexity than computational data. Much of big data is a by-product of everyday life. Big data needs qualitative researchers who have developed what Silverman (2013, p. 19) calls the "ethnographer's gaze"—a gaze that demands two things: "being able to locate the mundane features of extraordinary situations, and to identify what is remarkable in everyday life".

Big qualitative data can be distinguished in terms of whether the big data sets are created—that is, generated from participants for the purpose of the research—or found. Found data include existing organizational or administrative data, learning analytics, website dashboards, social media data, mobile phone data, and so on. Big qualitative data sets that are found often encounter some of the same problems as quantitative researchers who use repurposed data (Bisel et al., 2014), as described in Chapter 3, this volume.

Many qualitative researchers have a preference for data that is created or generated for research purposes. There is also a greater emphasis on understanding the conditions through which the data is produced and consumed, and how and why participants initiate, reflect upon, negotiate, delete, and curate the observed interactions. Bail (2014, p. 477) contends:

> Perhaps the most vexing problem is that big data often does not include information about the social context in which texts are produced...Although we are able to collect millions of blog posts about virtually any issue, these data typically include little or no information about the authors of such posts—or those who comment upon them.

Big qualitative research is in a strong position to examine the dimensions behind data production and online social action that cannot be explained by algorithms, dashboards, and screen scraping (Hand, 2014). For this reason, computational analysis of big data can be fruitfully complimented and enhanced by small data. Hand (2014, p. 23) suggests that

> In trying to situate data analytics (e.g., and the "quantified self") in this way, digital social research might provide much needed

Anticipating big data futures 59

detail about emerging alternative projects of self-knowledge, and the ways in which people...might use analytics "against the grain".

Despite the speed of mathematical computation performed by big data analytics, current quantitative analytic methods are not able to capture the subtlety, creativity, and personality that real human beings demonstrate across social contexts (Mills, 2017; Silver, 2012). Researchers cannot understand human behavior and social action without contextualizing the data and having information about the environment in which the data about social action occurs. This is why qualitative research has an important place to trace and probe the complex interactions between social action and context, as well as the subjectivity of human actors, whether dealing with big data, small data, or data sizes in-between (Mills, 2017).

An interesting way to think about big data from a qualitative vantage point is to recognize that we have data of increasing divisibility and smallness in terms of the constituent parts of each digital record. For example, video data can enable researchers to replay each microsecond of interactions, attending to the multifaceted multimodal features of a recorded social interaction, from each moment of varied body movement, head movement, posture, speech, gaze, facial expression, and so on. Cope and Kalantzis (2015, p. 208) elaborate on the smaller size of data points, "Smaller still might be a keystroke, a timestamp, a click in a navigation path, or a change captured in the edit history of a wiki or blog". The traceable and recorded by-products of digital interactions have become more atomic and can quickly add up. In other words, we have "more data than a human can deal with without computer-synthesized analytics" (Cope & Kalantzis, 2015, p. 208).

Social learning analytics has become a vital source of information about online learning communities (Cope & Kalantzis, 2015; Shum & Ferguson, 2012). For example, in higher education, online learning environments typically provide tools for collaborative knowledge work that draw on distributed cognition (Bohlouli, Dalter, Dornhöfer, Zenkert, & Fathi, 2015). Collaborative learning environments generate very large amounts of data produced collectively by learning teams, to which learning analytics can be applied (Cope & Kalantzis, 2015; Perera, Kay, Koprinska, Yacef, & Zaïane, 2009). A range of qualitative methods such as in-depth interviewing, discourse analysis, and content analysis have proved particularly useful in contextualizing various kinds of social data (boyd & Crawford, 2012), and which can be used to gain participant accounts and perspective of the collaborative aspects of learning environments. Small data research often utilizes mixed methods, combining analytics and surveys with qualitative techniques, such as participant observation and interviewing (Hand, 2014).

The richness and potential of big qualitative data has been realized in published research, such as the massive cross-national, longitudinal, narrative research described in Chapter 3, this volume. The research conducted by Winskell and colleagues (2018) involved the collection and analysis of a sample of almost 2, 000 narratives (n=1937) spanning various modes and media, from a total collection of 75,000 HIV-themed script-writing competition narratives. This study is a good example of how very large textual data analyzed both qualitatively and quantitatively can afford deep and expansive insights about youth sensemaking across varied sociocultural contexts. The development of research using big data sets with qualitative and mixed methods approaches has moved beyond rhetorical debates, with productive examples of methodologically thorough and theoretically substantiated practice emerging in different scholarly fields (Bancroft, Karels, Murray, & Zimpfer, 2014; Blok & Pedersen, 2014; O'Halloran, Tan, Pham, Bateman, & Vande Moere, 2018; Winskell et al., 2018).

The analytic methods and data management strategies applied in these studies have enabled the researchers to identify significant patterns across places and time, providing contextualized social or visual representations of the phenomenon or research problem of focus (Bancroft et al., 2014; Blok & Pedersen, 2014; O'Halloran et al., 2018; Winskell et al., 2018). Such big data studies have been used to build and analyze enormous and varied data sets without sacrificing the qualitative richness and description, and which have required highly original research designs. These studies were not ethically inferior to small studies, were no less contextualized, and the researchers made no claims to some kind of higher objectivity. Qualitative and mixed methods researchers can engage critically and creatively with emerging forms of big data that often require working in interdisciplinary ways to generate new social insights (Hand, 2014). Research change is intensifying so quickly that big data today may simply be data tomorrow.

References

Adams, M. (2017). Big data and individual privacy in the age of the internet of things. *Technology Innovation Management Review, 7*(4), 12–24.

Ajana, B. (2013). *Governing through biometrics: The biopolitics of identity*. Basingstoke, England: Palgrave Macmillan.

Ajana, B. (2015). Augmented borders: Big data and the ethics of immigration control. *Journal of Information, Communication and Ethics in Society, 13*(1), 58–78.

Alberts, B. (2012). The end of 'small science'? *Science, 337*(6102), 1583.

Allen, A. L. (2013). An ethical duty to protect one's own information privacy? *Alabama Law Review, 64*(4), 845–866.

Anderson, C. (2008). The end of theory: The data deluge makes the scientific method obsolete. *Wired*. Retrieved from http://www.wired.com/2008/06/pb-theory/

Andrejevic, M. (2013). *Infoglut: How too much information is changing the way we think and know*. New York, NY: Routledge.

Appadurai, A. (1990). Disjuncture and difference in the global cultural economy. *Theory, Culture & Society, 7*(2–3), 295–310.

Appadurai, A. (Ed.). (1986). *The social life of things: Commodities in cultural perspective*. New York, NY: Cambridge.

Bail, C. (2014). The cultural environment: Measuring culture with big data. *Theory and Society, 43*(3), 465–482.

Bancroft, A., Karels, M., Murray, O. M., & Zimpfer, J. (2014). Not being there: Research at a distance with video, text and speech. In M. Hand, & S. Hillyard (Eds.), *Big data? Qualitative approaches to digital research* (Vol. 13, pp. 137–153). Bingley, England: Emerald.

Banerjee, S. (2016). Sentiment analysis/opinion mining: Big data venturing into the new breed of data analysis. *Dataquest*. Retrieved from http://search.proquest.com/docview/1815383144/

Banner, D. J., & Albarrran, J. W. (2009). Computer-assisted qualitative data analysis software: A review. *Canadian Journal of Cardiovascular Nursing, 19*(3), 24–31.

Barbierato, E., Gribaudo, M., & Iacono, M. (2014). Performance evaluation of NoSQL big-data applications using multi-formalism models. *Future Generation Computer Systems, 27*(7), 345–353.

References

Barnaghi, P., Sheth, A., & Henson, C. (2013). From data to actionable knowledge: Big data challenges in the web of things. *IEEE Intelligent Systems, 28*(6), 6–11.

Barocas, S., & Nissenbaum, H. (2014). Big data's end run around anonymity and consent. In J. Lane, V. Stodden, S. Bender, & H. Nissenbaum (Eds.), *Privacy, big data and the public good: Frameworks for engagement* (pp. 44–75). New York, NY: Cambridge University Press.

Bassett, C. (2015). Plenty as a response to austerity? Big data expertise, cultures and communities. *European Journal of Cultural Studies, 18*(4–5), 548–563.

Baym, N. (2013). Data not seen: The uses and shortcomings of social media metrics. *First Monday, 18*(10), 1–15.

Bazeley, P. (2010). Computer assisted integration of mixed methods data sources and analyses. In A. Tashakkori & C. Teddlie (Eds.), *Sage handbook of mixed methods in social and behavioural research* (2nd ed., pp. 431–467). Thousand Oaks, CA: Sage.

Beauchamp, T. L., & Childress, J. F. (2013). *Principles of biomedical ethics* (7th ed.). New York, NY: Oxford University Press.

Beck, U. (1992). *Risk society: Towards a new modernity*. London, England: SAGE.

Bednarek, M. (2015). *Emotion talk across corpora*. London, England: Palgrave Macmillan.

Beer, D. (2012). Using social media data aggregators to do social research. *Sociological Research Online, 17*(3), 1–12.

Beer, D. (2016). How should we do the history of big data? *Big Data & Society, 3*(1), 1–10.

Bellinger, G. D., Castro, D., & Mills, A. (2004). Data, information, knowledge, and wisdom. Retrieved from http://www.systems-thinking.org/dikw/dikw.htm

Berlekamp, E. (2012). Small science: Radical innovation. *Science, 338*(6109), 882.

Berry, D. M. (2011). The computational turn: Thinking about the digital humanities. *Culture Machine, 12*, 1–22.

Berry, D. M. (2012). *Understanding digital humanities*. Basingstoke, England: Palgrave Macmillan.

Bezemer, J., & Kress, G. (2014). Touch: A resource for making meaning. *Australian Journal of Language and Literacy, 37*(2), 77–85.

Big data needs a hardware revolution. (2018). *Nature, 554*(7691), 145–146.

Bisel, R. S., Barge, J. K., Sougherty, D. S., Lucas, K., & Tracy, S. J. (2014). A round-table discussion of "big" data in qualitative organizational communication research. *Management Communication Quarterly, 28*(4), 625–649.

Blok, A., & Pedersen, M. A. (2014). Complementary social science? Qualiquantitative experiments in a big data world. *Big Data and Society, 1*(2), 1–6.

Bodenhamer, D. J., Corrigan, J., & Harris, T. (2010). *The spatial humanities: Gis and the future of humanities scholarship*. Bloomington: Indiana University Press.

Boehmke, B. C. (2016). *Data wrangling with R(Use R!)*. Dayton, OH: Springer International.

Bohlouli, M., Dalter, J., Dornhöfer, M., Zenkert, J., & Fathi, M. (2015). Knowledge discovery from social media using big data-provided sentiment analysis (somabit). *Journal of Information Science, 41*(6), 779–798.

References

Bollen, J., Mao, H., & Zeng, X. (2011). Twitter mood predicts the stock market. *Journal of Computational Science, 2*(1), 1–8.

Borgman, C. L. (2009). The digital future is now: A call to action for the humanities. *Digital Humanities Quarterly, 3*(4), 1–30.

Borgman, C. L. (2015). *Big data, little data, no data: Scholarship in the networked world* Cambridge, MA: MIT Press.

Borgman, C. L. (2018). Open data, grey data, and stewardship: Universities at the privacy frontier. *Berkeley Technology Law Journal, 33*(2), 1–39.

Borgman, C. L., Golshan, M. S., Sands, A. E., Wallis, J. C., Cummings, R. L., Darch, P. T., & Randles, B. M. (2016). Data management in the long tail: Science, software, and service. *International Journal of Digital Curation, 11*(1), 128–149.

Borgohain, T., Kuman, U., & Sanyal, S. (2015). Survey of security and privacy issues of Internet of things. *International Journal of Advanced Networking and Applications, 19*(11), 20–26.

boyd, d., & Crawford, K. (2011, September). Six provocations for big data. Paper presented at the Conference of the Oxford Internet Institute – A Decade in Internet Time: Symposium on the Dynamics of the Internet and Society, Oxford, England. Retrieved from: https://ssrn.com/abstract=1926431

boyd, d., & Crawford, K. (2012). Critical questions for big data: Provocations for a cultural, technological, and scholarly phenomenon. *Information, Communication & Society, 15*(5), 662–679.

Bruckman, A., Luther, K., & Fiesler, C. (2015). When should we use real names in published accounts of internet research? In E. Hargittai & C. Sandvig (Eds.), *Digital research confidential: The secrets of studying behavior online* (pp. 243–258). Cambridge, MA: MIT Press.

Burns, R. (2015). Rethinking big data in digital humanitarianism: Practices, epistemologies, and social relations. *Spatially Integrated Social Sciences and Humanities, 80*(4), 477–490.

Büscher, M., & Urry, J. (2009). Mobile methods and the empirical. *European Journal of Social Theory, 12*(1), 99–116.

Caliandro, A. (2014). Ethnography in digital spaces: Ethnography of virtual worlds, netnography, and digital ethnography. In R. Denny & P. Sunderland (Eds.), *Handbook of anthropology in business* (pp. 658–680). Walnut Creek, CA: Left Coast Press.

Camfield, L. (2018). Rigor and ethics in the world of big-team qualitative data: Experiences from research in international development. *American Behavioral Scientist*. doi:10.1177/0002764218784636

Chandler, D. (2015). A world without causation: Big data and the coming of age of posthumanism. *Millennium: Journal of International Studies, 43*(3), 833–851.

Cheek, J. (2004). At the margins? Discourse analysis and qualitative research. *Qualitative Health Research, 14*(8), 1140–1150.

Chen, M., Mao, S., & Liu, Y. (2014). Big data: A survey. *Mobile Networks and Applications, 19*(2), 171–209.

Christians, G., & Carey, J. W. (1989). The logics and aims of qualitative research. In G. H. I. Stempel & B. H. Westley (Eds.), *Research methods in mass communication* (pp. 354–374). Englewood Cliffs, NJ: Prentice Hall.

References

Clarke, A., & Margettes, H. (2014). Governments and citizens getting to know each other? Open, closed, and big data in public management reform. *Policy and Internet*, *6*(4), 393–497.

Clarke, R. (2016). Big data, big risks. *Information Systems Journal*, *26*(1), 77–90.

Community cleverness required (2008, September 3). *Nature*, *455*, 1. Retrieved from https://www.nature.com/collections/wwymlhxvfs

Cope, B., & Kalantzis, M. (2015). Sources of evidence-of-learning: Learning and assessment in the era of big data. *Open Review of Educational Research*, *2*(1), 194–217.

Coxon, T., Davies, P. M., Hunt, A. J., McManus, T. J., Rees, C. M., & Weatherburn, P. (1993). Research note: Strategies in eliciting sensitive sexual information: The case of gay men. *The Sociological Review*, *41*(3), 537–555.

Crompton, M. (2002). Biometrics and privacy. *Privacy Law and Policy Report*, *9*(3), 53–58.

Crossley, M. (2014). Global league tables, big data and the international transfer of educational research modalities. *Comparative Education*, *50*(1), 15–26.

Cukier, K. (2010, February). Data, data everywhere: A special report on managing information. *The Economist*. Retrieved from https://www.economist.com/node/15557443

D'Andrea, A., Ciolfi, L., & Gray, B. (2011). Methodological Challenges and Innovations in Mobilities Research. *Mobilities*, *6*(2), 149–160.

Daries, J., Reich, J., Waldo, J., Young, E., Whittinghill, J., Ho, A., ... Chuang, I. (2014). Privacy, anonymity, and big data in the social sciences. *Communications of the ACM*, *57*(9), 56–63.

Davenport, T. H., & Dyché, J. (2013). Big data in big companies. *International Institute for Analytics*. Retrieved from https://docs.media.bitpipe.com/io_10x/io_102267/item_725049/Big-Data-in-Big-Companies.pdf

Davenport, T. H., & Patil, D. (2012). Data scientist: The sexiest job of the 21st century. *Harvard Business Review*, *90*(5), 70–76.

De Solla Price, D. (1963). *Little science, big science and beyond*. New York, NY: Columbia University Press.

Dedić, N., & Stanier, C. (2017). *Towards differentiating business intelligence, big data, data analytics and knowledge discovery*. Berlin, Germany: Springer.

Dekas, K., & McCune, E. A. (2015). Conducting ethical research with big and small data: Key questions for practitioners. *Industrial and Organizational Psychology*, *8*(4), 563–567.

Delyser, D., & Sui, D. (2013). Crossing the qualitative-quantitative divide ii: Inventive approaches to big data, mobile methods, and rhythmanalysis. *Progress in Human Geography*, *37*(2), 293–305.

Desrosières, A. (2002). *The politics of large numbers: A history of statistical reasoning*. Cambridge, MA: Harvard University Press.

Economou, D. (2009). *Photos in the news: Appraisal analysis of visual semiosis and verbal-visual intersemiosis*. Sydney, Australia: University of Sydney.

Edensor, T. (2016a). Introduction: Thinking about geographies of rhythm and space. In T. Edensor (Ed.), *Geographies of rhythm: Nature, place, mobilities and bodies* (pp. 1–20). Abingdon, England: Routledge.

References 65

Edensor, T. (Ed.). (2016b). *Geographies of rhythm: Nature, place, mobilities and bodies*. Abingdon, England: Routledge.

El Alaoui, I., Gahi, Y., Messoussi, R., Chaabi, Y., Todoskoff, A., & Kobi, A. (2018). A novel adaptable approach for sentiment analysis on big social data. *Journal of Big Data, 5*(1), 1–18.

Elden, S. (2007). Governmentality, calculation, territory. *Environment and Planning D: Society and Space, 25*(3), 562–580.

Elliotte, A., & Urry, J. (2010). *Mobile lives*. Abingdon, England: Routlege.

Elwood, S., & Leszczynski, A. (2013). New spatial media, new knowledge politics. *Transactions of the Institute of British Geographers, 38*(4), 544–559.

Featherstone, M. (2000). Archiving cultures. *British Journal of Sociology, 51*(1), 168–184.

Foucault, M. (1977). *Discipline and punish: The birth of the prison* (A. Sheridan, Trans.). London, England: Penguin Books.

Foucault, M. (1997). What is critique? In S. Lotringer & L. Hochroth (Eds.), *The politics of truth* (pp. 41–82). New York, NY: Semiotext(e).

Foucault, M. (2007). *Security, territory, population: Lectures at the College de France 1977–1978*. Basingstoke, England: Palgrave Macmillan.

Friedman, U. (2012). Anthropology of an idea: Big data, a short history. *Foreign Policy, 196*, 30–31.

Frizzo-Barker, J., Chow-White, P. A., Mozafari, M., & Ha, D. (2016). An empirical study of the rise of big data in business scholarship. *International Journal of Information Management, 36*(3), 403–413.

Fuller, D., Buote, R., & Stanley, K. (2017). A glossary for big data in population and public health: Discussion and commentary on terminology and research methods. *Journal of Epidemiology and Community Health, 71*(11), 1113–1117.

Fuller, M. (2017). Big data, ethics and religion: New questions from a new science. *Religions, 8*(5), 88.

Gandomi, A., & Haider, M. (2015). Beyond the hype: Big data concepts, methods, and analytics. *International Journal of Information Management, 35*(2), 137–144.

Gibson, M. (2002). Doing a doctorate using a participatory action research framework in the context of community health. *Qualitative Health Research, 12*(4), 546–588.

Giddens, A. (1999). *Runaway world: How globalization is reshaping our lives*. London, England: Profile Books.

Ginsberg, J., Mohebbi, M. H., Patel, R. S., Brammer, L., Smolinski, M. S., & Brilliant, L. (2009). Detecting influenza epidemics using search engine query data. *Nature, 457*(7232), 1012–1015.

Golder, S. A., & Macy, M. W. (2011). Diurnal and seasonal mood vary with work, sleep, and day length across diverse cultures. *Science, 333*(6051), 1878–1881.

Graham, M., Hale, S., & Stephens, M. (2011). *Geographies of the world's knowledge*. London, England: Convoco.

Gregson, N., Crang, M., Ahamed, F., Akhter, N., & Ferdous, R. (2010). Following things of rubbish value: End-of-life ships, 'chock-chocky' furniture and the bangladeshi middle class consumer. *Geoforum, 41*(60), 846–854.

References

Grieco, M., & Urry, J. (Eds.). (2016). *Mobilities: New perspectives on transport and society*. Abingdon, England: Routledge.

Griswold, W., & Wright, N. (2004). Wired and well read. In S. Jones & P. N. Howard (Eds.), *Society online: The internet in context* (pp. 203–222). New York, NY: Sage.

Guetterman, T. C., Fetters, M. D., & Creswell, J. W. (2015). Integrating quantitative and qualitative results in health science mixed methods research through joint displays. *Annals of Family Medicine, 13*(6), 554–561.

Hacking, I. (Ed.). (1991). *How should we do the history of statistics?* Chicago, IL: The University of Chicago Press.

Halpern, O. (2015). *Beautiful data: A history of vision and reason since 1945*. Durham, NC: Duke University Press.

Hand, M. (2014). From cyberspace to the dataverse: Trajectories in digital social research. In M. Hand, S. Hillyard, C. Pole, & K. Love (Eds.), *Big data? Qualitative approaches to digital research* (Vol. 13, pp. 1–27). Bingley, England: Emerald.

Hand, M., Hillyard, S., Pole, C., & Love, K. (Eds.). (2014). *Big data? Qualitative approaches to digital research*. Bingley, England: Emerald.

Hashem, I. A. T., Yaqoob, I., Anuar, N. B., Mokhtar, S., Gani, A., & Khan, S. U. (2015). The rise of "big data" on cloud computing: Review and open research issues. *Information Systems, 47*, 98–115.

Hayes, A. (2014). Uberveillance: Where wear and educative arrangement. In M. G. Michael & K. Michael (Eds.), *Urbervillance the the social implications of microchip implants emerging technologies* (pp. 46–62). Hershey, PA: Information Science Reference.

Hayles, K. (2009). RFID: Human agency and meaning in information-intensive environments. *Theory, Culture & Society, 26*(2–3), 47–72.

Henry, C., Carnochan, S., & Austin, M. J. (2014). Using qualitative datamining for practice research in child welfare. *Child Welfare, 93*(6), 7–26.

Hey, T., Tansley, S., & Tolle, K. (2009). *The fourth paradigm: Data-intensive scientific discovery*. Redmond, WA: Microsoft Research.

Hine, C. (2000). *Virtual ethnography*. London, England: Sage.

Hoffmann, L. (2013). Looking back at big data. *Communications of the ACM, 56*(4), 21–23.

Hui, D. M. (2012). Things in motion, things in practices: How mobile practice networks facilitate the travel and use of leisure objects. *Journal of Consumer Culture, 12*(2), 195–215.

Ignatow, G., & Milhalcea, R. (2013). Text mining for comparative cultural analysis (Working Paper). Denton, TX: Department of Sociology, University of North Texas.

Investigatory Powers Act 2016 c.25 UK Parliament. Retrieved from http://www.legislation.gov.uk/ukpga/2018/12/schedule/19/part/1/crossheading/investigatory-powers-act-2016-c-25/2018-07-23

Ito, M., Horst, H. A., Bittanti, M., Boyd, D., Herr-Stevenson, B., Lange, P., … Robinson, L. (2008). *White paper: Living and learning with new media: Summary of findings from the digital youth project*. Retrieved from Chicago, IL: http://digitalyouth.ischool.berkeley.edu/report

References 67

Jaworski, A., & Thurlow, C. (2017). Gesture and movement in tourist spaces. In C. Jewitt (Ed.), *The Routledge handbook of multimodal analysis* (pp. 365–374). London, England: Routledge.

Jenkins, H., Clinton, K., Purushotma, R., Robinson, A., & Weigel, M. (2006). *Confronting the challenges of participatory culture: Media education for the 21st century*. Chicago, IL: MacArthur Foundation.

Jewitt, C. (2017). Introduction. In C. Jewitt (Ed.), *The Routledge handbook of multimodal analysis* (2nd ed., pp. 15–30). London, England: Routledge.

Kaisler, S., Armour, F., Espinosa, J. A., & Money, W. (2013, January). *Big data: Issues and challenges moving forward*. Paper presented at the 46th Hawaii International Conference on System Sciences, Hawaii.

Kim, G. H., Trimi, S., & Chung, J. H. (2014). Big-data applications in the government sector. *Communications of the ACM, 57*(3), 78–85.

King, G. (2011). Ensuring the data rich future of the social sciences. *Science, 331*(6018), 719–721.

Kirk, A. (2012). *Data visualization: A successful design process*. Birmingham, England: Packt.

Kitchin, R. (2013). Big data and human geography: Opportunities, challenges and risks. *Dialogues in human geography, 3*(3), 262–267.

Kitchin, R. (2014). *The data revolution: Big data, open data, data infrastructures and their consequences*. London, England: SAGE.

Knight, S., Shum, S., & Littleton, K. (2014). Epistemology, assessment, pedagogy: Where learning meets analytics in the middle space. *Journal of Learning Analytics, 1*(2), 23–47.

Koch, T., Selim, P., & Kralik, D. (2002). Enhancing lives through the development of a community-based particpatory action research program. *Journal of Clinical Nursing, 11*(1), 109–117.

Koonin, S. E., Steven, E., & Holland, M. J. (2014). The value of big data for urban science. In J. Lane, V. Stodden, S. Bender, & H. Nissenbaum (Eds.), *Privacy, big data and the public good: Frameworks for engagement* (pp. 137–152). New York, NY: Cambridge University Press.

Koppel, M., & Schler, J. (2006). The importance of neutral examples for learning sentiment. *Computational Intelligence, 22*(2), 100–109.

Kozinets, R. (2015). *Netnography redefined* (2nd ed.). London, England: SAGE.

Krishnamurthy, R., & Desouza, K. C. (2014). Big data analytics: The case of the social security administration. *Information Polity, 19*(3–4), 165–178.

Kuckartz, U. (2007). Qda-software im methodendiskurs: Geschichte, potenziale, effekte. In U. Kuckartz (Ed.), *Qualitative datenanalyse computergestützt: Methodische hintergründe und beispiele aus der forschungspraxis* (2nd ed., pp. 15–31). Wiesbaden: VS Verlag für Sozialwissenschaften.

Labrinidis, A., & Jagadish, H. V. (2012). Challenges and opportunities with big data. *Proceedings of the VLDB Endowment, 5*(12), 2032–2033.

Laney, D. (2001). 3D data management: Controlling data volume, velocity, and variety. *Application Delivery Strategies*. Stamford, CT: Meta Group.

Lash, S., & Lury, C. (2007). *Global culture industry: The mediation of things*. Cambridge, England: Polity Press.

References

Latour, B., Jensen, P., & Venturini, T. (2012). 'The whole is always smaller than its parts': A digital test of gabriel tarde's monads. *British Journal of Sociology, 63*(4), 590–615.

Lefebvre, H. (2004). *Rhythmanalysis: Space, time and everyday life*. London, England: Continuum.

Letouzé, E. (2012). Big data for development: Challenges and opportunities. *UN Global Pulse*, 1–47. Retrieved from http://www.unglobalpulse.org/sites/default/files/BigDataforDevelopment-UNGlobalPulseJune2012.pdf

Lohmeier, C. (2014). The researcher and the never-ending field: Reconsidering big data and digital ethnography. In M. Hand, & S. Hillyard (Eds.), *Big data? Qualitative approaches to digital research* (Vol. 13, pp. 75–89). Bingley, England: Emerald.

Lohr, S. (2012, February 12). The age of big data. *New York Times*. Retrieved from: https://www.nytimes.com/2012/02/12/sunday-review/big-datas-impact-in-the-world.html

Lyon, D. (2001). *Surveillance society: Monitoring everyday life*. Buckingham, England: Open University Press.

MacDonald, C. (2012). Understanding participatory action research: A qualitative research methodology option. *Canadian Journal of Action Research, 13*(2), 34–50.

Mai, J.-E. (2016). Big data privacy: The datafication of personal information. *The Information Society, 32*(3), 192–199.

Manovich, L. (2011). Trending: The promises and the challenges of big social data. *Debates in the digital humanities, 2*, 460–475.

Marciano, R. J., Allen, R. C., Hou, C.-Y., & Lach, P. R. (2013). "Big historical data" feature extraction. *Journal of Map & Geography Libraries, 9*(1–2), 69–80.

Marcus, G. E. (1995). Ethnography in/of the world system: The emergence of multisited ethnography. *Annual Review of Anthropology, 24*, 95–117.

Martin, J. R., & White, P. R. R. (2005). *The language of evaluation: Appraisal in English*. New York, NY: MacMillan.

Marwick, A. E. (2014). Ethnographic and qualitative research on Twitter. In K. Weller, A. Bruns, J. Burgess, M. Mahrt, & C. Puschmann (Eds.), *Twitter and society* (pp. 109–122). New York, NY: Peter Lang.

Mayer-Schönberger, V., & Cukier, K. (2013). *Big data: A revolution that will transform how we live, work, and think*. Boston, MA: Houten, Mifflin, and Harcourt.

McFarland, D., Lewis, C., & Goldberg, A. (2016). Sociology in the era of big data: The ascent of forensic social science. *The American Sociologist, 47*(1), 12–35.

Melles, G. (2004). Smartphone ethnography/ethnomethodology for design. *European Journal of Information Systems, 13*(3), 195–209.

Meyer, E. T. (2009). Moving from small science to big science: Social and organizational impediments to large scale data sharing. In N. Jankowski (Ed.), *E-research: Transformations in scholarly practice* (pp. 147–159). New York, NY: Routledge.

Michael, M. G., & Michael, K. (2014). *Uberveillance and the social implications of microchip implants emerging technologies*. Hershey, PA: Information Science Reference.

References 69

Michel, J. B., Shen, Y. K., Aiden, A. P., Veres, A., Gray, M. K., & Pickett, J. P. (2010). Quantitative analysis of culture using millions of digitized books. *Science, 331*(6014), 176–182.

Mills, K. A. (2010). A review of the digital turn in the new literacy studies. *Review of Educational Research, 80*(2), 246–271.

Mills, K. A. (2016, 27–29 September). *What children's photography can teach us about affect, judgement and appreciation.* Paper presented at the Australian Systemic Functional Linguistics Association, Sydney, Australia.

Mills, K. A. (2017). What are the threats and potentials of big data for qualitative research? *Qualitative Research, Online first,* 1–13. doi:10.1177/14687 94117743465

Mills, K. A., & Comber, B. (2015). Socio-spatial approaches to literacy studies: Rethinking the social constitution and politics of space. In K. Pahl & J. Rowsell (Eds.), *Handbook of literacy studies* (pp. 91–103). London, England: Routledge.

Mills, K. A., & Unsworth, L. (2017). Multimodal literacy. In G. Noblit (Ed.), *Oxford research encyclopedia of education.* Oxford, England: Oxford Univeristy Press.

Mills, K. A., & Unsworth, L. (2018). Ipad animations: Powerful multimodal practices for adolescent literacy and emotional language. *Journal of Adolescent & Adult Literacy, 61*(6), 609–620.

Mills, K. A., Unsworth, L., Bellocchi, A., Park, J.-Y., & Ritchie, S. M. (2014). Children's multimodal appraisal of places: Walking with the camera. *Australian Journal of Language and Literacy, 37*(3), 171–181.

Milton, C. L. (2017). The ethics of big data and nursing science. *Nursing Science Quarterly, 30*(4), 300–302.

Mitchell, G. (2018). What is meant by the term 'geoweb'? *Science Focus: BBC Focus Magazine.* London, England: BBC Studios.

Montgomery, K. (2015). Children's media culture in a big data world. *Journal of Children and Media, 9*(2), 266–271.

Murphey, K. P. (2012). *Machine learning, a probabilistic perspective.* Cambridge, MA: MIT Press.

Murray, L. (2009). Looking at and looking back: Visualisation in mobile research. *Qualitative Research, 9*(4), 469–488.

Murthy, D. (2008). Digital ethnography: An examination of the use of new technologies for social research. *Sociology, 42*(5), 837–855.

Nardulli, P. F., Althaus, S. L., & Hayes, M. (2015). A progressive, supervised-learning approach to generating rich civil strife data. *Sociological Methodology, 45*(1), 148–183.

Nath, S., Liu, J., & Zhao, F. (2007). Sensormap for wide-area sensor webs. *Embedded computing, 40*(7), 90–93.

O'Brien, D. T., Sampson, R. J., & Winship, C. (2015). Ecometrics in the age of big data: Measuring and assessing "broken windows" using large-scale administrative records. *Sociological Methodology, 45*(1), 101–147.

O'Donohoe, S. (2010). Netnography: Doing ethnographic research online. *International Journal of Advertising, 29*(2), 328–330.

O'Halloran, K. L., Tan, S., Pham, D., Bateman, J., & Vande Moere, A. (2018). A digital mixed methods research design: Integrating multimodal analysis with data mining and information visualization for big data analytics. *Journal of Mixed Methods Research, 12*(1), 11–30.

Parks, M. R. (2014). Big data in communication research: Its contents and discontents. *Journal of Communication, 64*(2), 355–360.

Paul, M. J., & Dredze, M. (2011). You are what you tweet: Analyzing twitter for public health. *Icwsm, 20*, 265–272.

Perera, C., Ranjan, R., Wang, L., Khan, S. U., & Zomaya, A. Y. (2015). Big data privacy in the internet of things era. *IT Professional, 17*(3), 32–39.

Perera, D., Kay, J., Koprinska, I., Yacef, K., & Zaïane, O. R. (2009). Clustering and sequential pattern mining of online collaborative learning data. *IEEE Transactions on Knowledge and Data Engineering, 21*(6), 759–772.

Philip, H., & Bilyana, P. (2017). Reining in the big promise of big data: Transparency, inequality, and new regulatory frontiers. *Northwestern Journal of Technology and Intellectual Property, 15*(1), 1–74.

Pokorny, J., Norman, A., Zanesco, A., Bauer-Wu, S., Sahdra, B. K., & Saron, C. D. (2016). Network analysis for the visualization and analysis of qualitative data. *Psychological Methods, 23*(1), 169–183.

Porter, T. M. (1986). *The rise of statistical thinking: 1820–1900*. Princeton, NJ: Princeton University Press.

Postill, J., & Pink, S. (2012). Social media ethnography: The digital researcher in a messy web. *Media International Australia, 145*(1), 123–134.

Puri, A. (2007). The web of insights: The art and practice of webnography. *International Journal of Market Research, 49*(3), 387–408.

Qiu, J. L. (2015). Reflections on big data: 'Just because it is accessible does not make it ethical'. *Media, Culture & Society, 37*(7), 1089–1094.

Ragini, J. R., Anand, P. M. R., & Bhaskar, V. (2018). Big data analytics for disaster response and recovery through sentiment analysis. *International Journal of Information Management, 42*, 13–24.

Raley, R. (2013). Dataveillance and countervaillance. In L. Gitelman (Ed.), *Raw data is an oxymoron* (pp. 121–145). Cambridge, MA and London, England: MIT Press.

Rasid, N., Nohuddin, P. E., Alias, H., Hamzah, I., & Nordin, A. I. (2017). *Using data mining strategy in qualitative research*. Paper presented at the Advances in Visual Informatics, Cham, Switzerland.

Regulating the internet giants: The world's most valuable resource is no longer oil, but data. (2017, May 6). *The Economist*. Retrieved from https://www.economist.com/leaders/2017/05/06/the-worlds-most-valuable-resource-is-no-longer-oil-but-data

Reips, U., & Garaizar, P. (2013). *Iscience maps*. Bilbao, Spain: University of Deusto.

Rghioui, A., Aziza, L., Elouaai, F., & Bouhorma, M. (2015). Protecting e-healthcare data privacy for internet of things based wireless body area network. *Research Journal of Applied Sciences, Engineering and Technology, 9*(10), 876–885.

Rockwell, G., & Berendt, B. (2016). On big data and text mining in the humanities. In S. ElAtia, D. Ipperciel, & O. Zaïane (Eds.), *Data mining and learning*

References 71

analytics: Applications in educational research (pp. 29–40). Hoboken, NJ: Wiley-Blackwell.

Ronksley-Pavia, M., & Barton, G. (2017). Early adolescent engagement with multimodal literacies. Paper presented at the Australian Association for Research in Education, Canberra, Australia.

Rosenberg, D. (2013). Data before the fact. In L. Gitelman (Ed.), *Raw data is an oxymoron* (pp. 15–40). Cambridge, MA: The MIT Press.

Rust, H. (2017). Virtuelle bilderwolken: Eine qualitative big data-analyse der geschmackskulturen im internet. Springer: VS Verlag für Sozialwissenschaften.

Sawyer, S. (2008). Data wealth, data poverty, data science and cyber infrastructure. *Prometheus, 26*(4), 355–371.

Schermer, B. W., Custer, B., & van der Hof, S. (2014). The crisis of consent: How stronger legal protection may lead to weaker consent in data protection. *Ethics and Information Technology, 16*(2), 171–182.

Sen, R., & Borle, S. (2015). Estimating the contextual risk of data breach: An empirical approach. *Journal of Management Information Systems, 32*(2), 314–341.

Shayaa, S., Jaafar, N. I., Bahri, S., Sulaiman, A., Wai, P. S., Chung, Y. W., ... Al-Garadi, M. A. (2018). Sentiment analysis of big data: Methods, applications, and open challenges. *IEEE Access, 6*, 37807–37827.

Shlomo, N., & Goldstein, H. (2015). Big data in social research. *Journal of the Royal Statistical Society: Series A (Statistics in Society), 178*(4), 787–790.

Shum, S. B., & Ferguson, R. (2012). Social learning analytics. *Journal of Educational Technology & Society, 15*(3), 3–26.

Sieber, R. E., Wellen, C. C., & Jin, Y. (2011). Spatial cyberinfrastructures, ontologies, and the humanities. *Proceedings of the National Academy of Science, 108*(14), 5504–5509.

Siegel, E. (2013). *Predictive analytics: The power to predict who will click, buy, lie, or die*. Hoboken, NJ: John Wiley and Sons.

Silver, N. (2012). *The signal and the noise: Why so may predications fail – but some don't*. New York, NY: Penguin Press.

Silverman, D. (2013). *A very short, fairly interesting and reasonably cheap book about qualitative research*. London, England: Sage.

Silverman, D. (2015). *Interpreting qualitative data* (5th ed.). London, England: Sage.

Sivarajah, U., Kamal, M. M., Irani, Z., & Weerakkody, V. (2017). Critical analysis of big data challenges and analytical methods. *Journal of Business Research, 70*, 263–286.

Smith, A., Cope, B., & Kalantzis, M. (2017). The quantified writer. In K. Mills, A. Stornaiuolo, J. Z. Pandya, & A. Smith (Eds.), *Handbook of writing, literacies, and education in digital cultures* (pp. 235–247). New York, NY: Taylor & Francis.

Smith, R. J. (2014). Missed miracles and mystical connections: Qualitative research, digital social science and big data. In M. Hand, & S. Hillyard (Eds.), *Big data? Qualitative approaches to digital research* (Vol. 13, pp. 181–204). Bingley, England: Emerald.

References

Snijders, C., Matzat, U., & Reips, U. (2012). Big data: Big gaps of knowledge in the field of internet science. *International Journal of Internet Science, 7*(1), 1–5.

Solove, D. J. (2013). Privacy management and the consent dilemma. *Harvard Law Review, 126*(7), 1880–1903.

Special online collection: Dealing with data. (2011, February 11). *Science*. Retrieved from https://www.sciencemag.org/site/special/data/

Stoller, P. (2013). Big data, thick description and political expediency. *Huffington Post*. Retrieved from https://www.huffingtonpost.com/paul-stoller/big-data-thick-descrption_b_3450623.html

Stopczynski, A., Sekara, V., & Sapiezynski, P. (2014). Measuring large-scale social networks with high resolution. *PLoS ONE, 9*(4), 1–24.

Strong, C. (2013). The challenge of big data: What does it mean for the qualitative research industry? *Qualitative Market Research: An International Journal, 14*(7), 336–343.

Sunderland, N., Bristed, H., Gudes, O., Boddy, J., & Da Silva, M. (2012). What does it feel like to live here? Exploring sensory ethnography as a collaborative methodology for investigating social determinants of health in place. *Health and Place, 18*(5), 1056–1067.

Sweeney, L. (2002). K-anonymity: A model for protecting privacy. *International Journal on Uncertainty, Fuzziness and Knowledge-based Systems, 10*(5), 557–570.

Szalai, A. (1972). *The use of time: Daily activities of urban and suburban populations in twelve countries*. Mouton, Netherlands: Den Haag.

Tay, L., Ng, V., Malik, A., Zhang, J., Chae, J., Ebert, D. S., ... Kern, M. (2017). Big data visualizations in organizational science. *Organizational Research Methods, 21*(3), 660–688.

Thelwall, M., Buckley, K., Paltoglou, G., & Cai, D. (2010). Sentiment strength detection in short informal text. *Journal of the American Society for Information Science and Technology, 61*(12), 2544–2558.

Thrift, N. (2005). *Knowing capitalism*. London, England: Sage.

Todd, R. J. (2008). Youth and their virtual networked worlds: Research findings and implications for school libraries. *School Libraries Worldwide, 14*(2), 19–34.

Troisi, O., Grimaldi, M., Loia, F., & Maione, G. (2018). Big data and sentiment analysis to highlight decision behaviours: A case study for student population. *Behaviour & Information Technology, 37*(10–11), 1–18.

Trottier, D. (2014). Big data ambivalence: Visions and risks in practice. In M. Hand & S. Hillyard (Eds.), *Big data? Qualitative approaches to digital research* (Vol. 13, pp. 51–72). Bingley, England: Emerald Group Publishing Limited.

Truyens, N., & Van Eecke, P. (2014). Legal aspects of text mining. *Computer Law and Security Review, 30*(2), 153–170.

Vaitsis, C., Nilsson, G., & Zary, N. (2014). Visual analytics in healthcare education: Exploring novel ways to analyze and represent big data in undergraduate medical education. *PeerJ, 2*, 1–17.

References 73

Wang, T. (2013). Big data needs thick data. *Ethnography Matters*. Retrieved from http://ethnographymatters.net/blog/2013/05/13/big-data-needs-thick-data/

Wenzel, R., & Van Quaquebeke, N. (2018). The double-edged sword of big data in organizational and management research: A review of opportunities and risks. *Organizational Research Methods, 21*(3), 548–591.

Wiedemann, G. (2013). Opening up to big data: Computer-assisted analysis of textual data in social sciences. *Forum: Qualitative Social Research, 14*(2), 311–320.

Wiedemann, G. (2016). *A study on democratic discourse in germany*. Wiesbaden, Germany: Springer.

Wilbanks, J. (2014). Portable approaches to informed consent and open data. In J. Lane, V. Stodden, S. Bender, & H. Nissenbaum (Eds.), *Privacy, big data and the public good: Frameworks for engagement* (pp. 234–252). New York, NY: Cambridge University Press.

Williams, E. N., & Morrow, S. L. (2009). Achieving trustworthiness in qualitative research: A panparadigmatic perspective. *Psychotherapy Research, 19*(4–5), 576–582.

Willis, J. (2016). Satellite surveillance and outer-space capitalism: The case of Macdonald, Dettwiler and associates. In P. Dickens & J. S. Ormrod (Eds.), *The Palgrave handbook of society, culture and outer space* (pp. 94–122). New York, NY: Palgrave Handbooks.

Winskell, K., Singleton, R., & Sabben, G. (2018). Enabling analysis of big, thick, long, and wide data: Data management for the analysis of a large longitudinal and cross-national narrative data set. *Qualitative Health Research, 28*(10), 1629–1639.

Yi, X., Liu, F., Liu, J., & Jin, H. (2014). Building a network highway for big data: Architecture and challenges. *IEEE Network, 28*(4), 5–13.

Yu, Y., & Wang, X. (2015). World Cup 2014 in the Twitter World: A big data analysis of sentiments in U.S. Sports fans' tweets. *Computers in Human Behavior, 48*, 392–400.

Index

access (to data) 8, 11, 13, 27–30, 52
administrative data 6, 37, 58
AI. *see* artificial intelligence (AI)
algorithms 25, 31, 35, 39, 40, 52, 58
analytics 4, 6–9, 11, 12, 14, 18, 22, 23, 26, 32–48, 50, 54–60
anonymized data 29, 54
archiving 2, 4, 19, 20
artificial intelligence (AI) 32, 38
arts and humanities 34
ATLAS.ti 36
audio data 8, 10, 32, 45

BDA *see* big data analytics (BDA)
big data: assumptions 3, 8, 12–14, 21, 57; by-product of social interaction 1, 56; challenges 8, 10, 11, 22–33; coining 18–19; debates 1, 2, 4, 8, 10, 17, 18, 23, 37, 60; definitions 9–11, 58; examples 3, 11, 13, 17; exclusion 56; fields of use 7, 37; geographical trends 26; history of 17, 18, 21; limitations 4, 56; mixed methods research 2, 3, 8, 24, 34, 41, 60; narrative 17, 20, 23, 32, 33, 37, 40, 48; naturally-occurring 20, 23, 27, 49; potentials 2, 4, 6, 8, 9, 12, 18, 25, 28, 30, 34–48, 53, 60; qualitative research 2–4, 7, 8, 14–15, 17, 20, 22–4, 28, 33, 35–7, 41–3, 48, 57–9; structured 9, 10, 32, 57; unstructured 9, 10, 23, 32, 35, 37, 38, 40, 42, 48, 57; value 3, 5, 14, 30, 32, 47; variety 9, 10, 26, 32, 47; velocity 9, 10, 29, 32, 47; veracity 10; volume 9, 10, 12, 17, 32, 47

big data acquisition 27–31
big data analytics (BDA) 4, 9, 22, 23–6, 31–48, 59
big data divides: age 29, 33, 34, 50, 54; dis/abilities 50; Indigenous 30; natural disasters 13, 30, 49; poverty 28; remote 30
big qualitative research 58
big science 17

CAQDA *see* computer-assisted qualitative data analysis (CAQDA)
collaborative learning environments 59
computer-assisted qualitative data analysis (CAQDA) 37–8, 47, 48
computer scientist 2, 14, 35
consumer behaviour forecasting 50
content analysis 11, 36, 38, 59
critical practice 55
cross-national research 60
cultural geography 47
culturomics 36

dashboard (analytics) 24, 32, 37, 52, 58
data: bias 14, 30; breaches 50; cleaning 18, 31; cross-national 32, 60; definition 16; de-identification 53; hardware and infrastructure 1, 2, 22, 26; integration 31, 41; longitudinal 17, 32, 60; machine-enabled 22; misuse 30; narrative 17, 20, 23, 32, 33, 37, 40, 48; naturalistic 20; numerical 8–10, 41; ownership 8, 13, 18, 27, 49, 53; participatory 24; privacy 18, 23, 27, 29, 49–56; qualitative 7, 9, 20, 23, 30, 36, 37,

40, 41, 57, 58, 60; rare 5, 8, 30; raw 31, 35, 36, 40; security 2, 27, 47, 51; semantics 31; software 1, 22, 40; structure 26, 31; visualization 7, 9, 22, 34, 35, 40–1, 48
database design 31
data driven decision-making 56
datafication 51
Data-Information-Knowledge-Wisdom (DIKW) pyramid 51
data mining 6, 7, 19, 22, 31, 32, 36, 41, 56
data scientist 22, 31
dataveillance 49–56
de-identification of data 53, 54
digital data 6, 8, 10–12, 19, 23, 25, 27, 30, 32–4, 40, 42, 45, 46, 48, 52, 53
digital footprint 30, 51, 56
digital humanities 12, 34, 36
digital turn 18
digitization 4, 32
DIKW pyramid *see* Data-Information-Knowledge-Wisdom (DIKW) pyramid
distributed cognition 59
divisibility of big data 59
document data 35

embargos 28
emotions (analysis) 38, 39, 45
ethical concerns 44, 49, 56
ethics principles for research 53, 56
ethnographic gaze 58
ethnography: digital 42; mobile 42; multisite 24, 43; sensory 45; smartphone 42; virtual 42; web 42

fake news 27
flows (data) 24, 45–7
follow-the-thing methods 34, 43–4
function creep 53

gatekeepers 29
geospatial data 20, 44
geospatial web 44
Giddens, A. 49
global mobilities 44
governance and big data 16, 19, 23, 27, 56
GPS trackers 11, 43

health monitoring 52
heterogenous data 32, 34
humanities 2.0 34
human resources (for big data analytics) 31
human subjectivity 59

identity theft 50
ideology 1, 19, 38, 48, 57
informational privacy 50
internet giants 29, 30
Internet of Things (IoT) 11, 43, 46, 51
interviews (in qualitative research) 2, 7, 23–5, 37, 40, 45
Investigatory Powers Act 2016 (UK) 51
IoT *see* Internet of Things (IoT)

k-anonymity 53, 54
knowledge politics 21

learning analytics 11, 12, 58, 59
little science 17
location-based services 43, 44
longitudinal research 44
long tail metaphor 26
long term data storage 53

machine learning 6, 9, 11, 32, 38, 39
manufactured risk 49
Massive Open Online Courses (MOOCs) 29, 53
material life of things 43
MAX 36
MAXQDA 36
mixed methods research 8, 24, 34, 38, 41
mobile data 32, 42
mobile research methods 34, 44–5, 47, 48
modes 9, 19, 23, 24, 26, 34, 39, 45, 46, 60
MOOCs *see* Massive Open Online Courses (MOOCs)
multimodal 4, 8, 19, 20, 39, 41, 46, 59; analysis 22, 34, 39, 45–7; semiotics 41, 44, 45

national data repositories 30
naturalistic inquiry 23
natural language processing (NLP) 11, 35, 36, 38

netnography 34, 41–2, 47, 48
networked data 3, 10
NLP *see* natural language processing (NLP)
NUD*IST software 36
Nvivo 36

online data 27
online identities 27
online opinion 40
open access data 28, 31, 32
open vocabulary analysis 36
opinion mining 11, 34, 38–40, 48

participant observation 3, 15, 24, 41, 42, 45, 60
participatory action research 23
predictive analytics 11, 50, 54, 57
privacy (and big data): legislation 23; research concerns 8, 27, 49, 52; risks 49
property rights 52
proprietary data 28
public awareness 27
public engagement with digital technology 27
public-private dichotomy 50

qualitative analysis 20, 23, 25, 36
qualitative coding 4, 36, 41
qualitative research 2–4, 7, 8, 14–15, 17, 20, 22–4, 28, 33, 35–7, 41–3, 48, 57–9
quantitative research 14, 47

radio frequency identification (RFID) tags 43, 52
repurposed data 58
research ethics 28, 53, 56
RFID tags *see* radio frequency identification (RFID) tags

rhythm (researching) 46, 47
rhythmanalysis 34, 46–7

screen scraping 11, 58
secondary use of data 28
semantic maps 36
sensitive data 28
sensor data 6, 37
sentiment analysis 6, 9, 11, 22, 34, 38–40
sharing data 4, 23, 27, 41, 49, 53, 56
small data research 14, 59–60
snooper's charter 51
social context in big data research 14, 49, 58, 59
social learning analytics 59
social media 6, 10, 11, 24, 27–9, 32, 34, 35, 40–2, 46, 49, 53; companies 29; data 6, 24, 29, 30, 53, 58
social network analysis 24, 42
socio-cultural factors (big data analysis) 33, 39, 60
sociology and big data 12, 13
speed of computation 59
statistics 18, 19, 29, 30

technological rationalization 49
text mining 22, 34–9
textual data 2, 7, 10, 16–21, 23, 32, 35, 37, 38, 40–2, 46, 60
thick data 15
triangulation 54, 58

uberveillance 52

video data 7, 45, 59
videography 42
visual data 32, 58
visualization (of data and information) 40–1

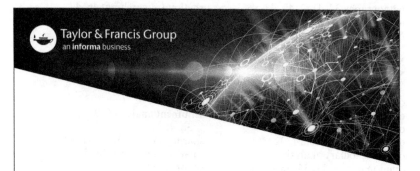